The Basics of Mastering ClickUp

Get Up and Running in No Time

Yvonne Heimann

ClickUp Evangelist & Consultant

Business Alignment Coach

AskYvi.com

Ask Yvi
Yvonne Heimann
4142 Adams Ave 103-441
San Diego, CA 92116
AskYvi.com

First Edition
ISBN: 9798375964201

DEDICATION

To all that have made this book happen,
starting all the way back with an idea back in 2021.

One non-aligned pitch, a crappy publishing house,
and quite a rollercoaster later... we made it!

This book exists because of YOU!

Your support.
Your belief in me.

Thank you

...and a HUGE thank you to Kitty and the team,
without you this book would not exist.

FOREWORD by Zeb Evans, founder & CEO at ClickUp

I died 5 times. Almost.

Each near death experience taught me how valuable, or maybe priceless, time is.

At the end of the day, and at the end of life, our life is a compilation of where we chose to spend our time.

No one's holding a gun to your head is a common saying that didn't mean much to me until my second near-death experience, where I literally had a gun held to my head during a home invasion. It was the first moment I ever had true clarity on what time really means.

The first thing I learned coming out of that experience, alive and unharmed, was the importance of how we choose to spend our time on earth. The second thing I walked away with was a burning question: how can I do everything I want and need to do, but in less time?

I became a productivity junky. I hacked daily routines like journaling and meditation, but also vowed to use all of the tools I could get my hands on to save time.

When I met Alex (ClickUp's technical mastermind), we were going to build a new Craigslist. Before we got started, we pledged to build the product in the most efficient way possible. We wouldn't waste any time.

We ended up with 15 different "productivity" tools that all did one thing we needed. There was a slight problem, though. I couldn't shake the feeling that using so many different productivity tools wasn't productive.

That's when we decided to build our own productivity tool. We initially thought it would just be for internal use to save ourselves time. Within weeks, we were obsessed. We had found our purpose - to save the world time.

The original ClickUp vision is the same today: one place for all of your work. We save time without losing context, switching between apps, and managing separate workflows in different places.

Since day one, we relied on our community to help us build the product. Yvi was an early community supporter who was obsessed with efficiency just like me. She played a critical role in building the community and teaching others how to best use ClickUp.

It's only fitting that the first ClickUp book be written by Yvi. Her book is a gift to the world - an opportunity for everyone to learn how they can save their most precious resource: time.

Let's make the world more productive, together.

 Zeb

Table of Contents

Introduction

What a journey it has been, and it goes way back in 2018 when my frustration with Asana's limited capabilities led me to explore better options (*Did you know? To this day, they still only allow 1 assignee per task*).

I vividly remember going LIVE on Facebook, coming up with a rather unpolished video to my community about this cool new tool I found called, 'ClickUp'. Who would have known that this encounter would mark the beginning of this epic journey?

Really, a lot has happened since then... I went on to produce hundreds of training videos. Guiding ClickUp users all over the world on setup techniques, and even collaborated with fellow content creators to find the holy grail of project management (*which, in my case, will always be ClickUp!*). I've also had the privilege of consulting and coaching hundreds of businesses on developing airtight processes, helping them implement more streamlined workflows, and using ClickUp to tie it all together seamlessly.

Working with all sorts of businesses showed me that there's still a huge gap when it comes to training teams on how to master the basics of ClickUp. And you might be curious why this is the case, when there is no shortage of tutorials online – there's ClickUp University, YouTube, and other paid courses for example.

To close this gap, I dedicated my time to creating custom ClickUp training sessions to suit my clients' specific needs. This tailored approach helped ensure that the features we implement perfectly align with their unique organizational requirements; enabling the development of standard operating procedures, along with the streamlining of any ongoing or future team and client onboarding.

But there's bound to be a limit to how many businesses I can help with those custom 1:1 training, right?

Prior to this book, most online resources consisted of lengthy training videos, or user cases that might not be easy to replicate for non-traditional business types. Given the hectic schedules of team members, expecting them to dedicate time to videos ranging from 15 to 60 minutes proved impractical.

"What if you could Master the Basics of ClickUp without having to sit and sift through hundreds of hours of content?"

Thus, the concept for this book was born.

A ClickUp book that can be easily handed out to teams and key members, offering a deep dive into best use scenarios. To put it simply, my goal is to cover the basics comprehensively, so that no one in your organization gets left behind.

Now, I know that this book is not a one-size-fits-all solution, so we've included a membership called, **StartUp Your ClickUp**. It complements this book with weekly office hours for all your questions.

Enjoy your first 2 months absolutely free by signing up here: http://askyvi.tips/MCU2

And while having access to a multitude of resources is valuable, it's important to remember that building a resilient and sustainable business relies on the systems and processes you implement. Because the truth is, ClickUp itself is not the answer to all your problems - it's YOU, you are the secret sauce to your success!

Proficiency in ClickUp helps you to implement better processes and strategies without unnecessary delays. This book aims to equip you with the knowledge needed to grasp ClickUp's best-used features, allowing you to develop your internal project management system with ease and confidence.

Are you ready to dive in?

Join me and let's Master the Basics of ClickUp one chapter at a time.

For all supporting and bonus resources go to: https://askyvi.tips/SPMCBonus

CHAPTER 1

Navigating Your ClickUp Workspace

C lickUp transcends basic task management, elevating your project management capabilities far beyond a simple to-do list. Envision the endless possibilities for yourself, your business, and your team! With this guide in your hands, navigating ClickUp's features will become second nature, making productivity and efficiency a seamless experience.

In this book, you will learn how to:

- Effectively manage tasks and teams
- Add and utilize data efficiently
- Unlock advanced features
- Customize ClickUp to your liking

However, having all this functionality right at your fingertips can be overwhelming. The primary goal of this book, especially within this chapter, is to explore the fundamental aspects of ClickUp, demystify its core features, and make them more accessible.

You will learn about the following topics:

- Setting up your ClickUp Workspace
- ClickUp hierarchy
- Views and how to use them
- Tasks and their features

By the chapter's end, you'll understand ClickUp's features and how to construct a strong, scalable setup.

Even if you already have a basic understanding of ClickUp, I recommend reading this chapter. In my numerous consulting sessions, I have seen that even the most advanced ClickUp users often don't know everything there is to know – especially when it comes to the most basic features.

For the best experience, follow along on your laptop or desktop using the ClickUp browser app to ensure you have the most up-to-date version; although the mobile and desktop apps are useful, they come with some limitations.

Setting up your ClickUp Workspace

Initiating the sign-up process for your ClickUp workspace is straightforward. Visit https://askyvi.com/clickup (yes, that is my affiliate link) and select the Sign Up button located at the top right of the website. This action initiates the onboarding process, leading you through a set of questions to personalize your ClickUp workspace.

If you already have a ClickUp account, this will direct you to the browser app.

Signing up for ClickUp

After clicking the Sign Up button, the site will walk you through the steps of entering your email address, setting your password, and adding your name. The email provided should be associated with the owner of the new ClickUp workspace. The name you enter will serve as your screen name in ClickUp, and the password will be used for future logins.

Following the basic information, ClickUp will prompt you with a series of questions to configure your workspace's appearance. The onboarding process also facilitates the addition of team members and the importation of tasks from your previous project management tool.

Here are some things to consider in the process of creating your workspace:

- I typically advise against exporting tasks from your previous project management system and directly importing them into ClickUp. Since project management systems have different structures, importing without considering these structural differences can lead to complications. Moving from your old project management tool to ClickUp is the perfect time to re-evaluate your process. Think of it as a good spring cleaning for your workflows!

Once your ClickUp workspace is set up, you can still import from a different task management tool through the Import/Export tab in your workspace settings.

- Consider who in your team should or shouldn't be invited to your new ClickUp workspace early on. Given the time spent setting things up and learning the platform, it's worth contemplating whether all team members should be involved right from the start.

- I highly recommend completing the basic setup alone or with key stakeholders like your business manager or ClickUp consultant. Once the initial setup is done, you can invite the rest of your team to join. This approach helps create a smoother onboarding process and allows for a more organized introduction of team members to the workspace.

When you first sign up, you will be on the Free Forever plan. Let's take a look at what other plans there are and how they compare.

Understanding ClickUp plans, pricing, and how to upgrade

ClickUp has a Free Forever plan, three regular user and Business plans, and one Enterprise plan. Each of these plans has its own set of features and capabilities. Before we dive deeper into the differences in the plans, let's look at how seats, also known as users, are handled in ClickUp.

People in ClickUp are either Full Members or Guests.

Full Members can have different user roles. There's the Owner user role; there is also an Admin role, Member, as well as custom roles. For the sake of keeping this book simple we'll stay away from custom roles as they are an advanced feature and really only come to play in bigger agency-type setups.

Here's a closer look into how these users are handled when you are on a paid account.

Users in a paid account

Your Guest seats in ClickUp are based on which ClickUp plan you are on and how many Full Members are part of your workspace.

For example:

- If you are on the Unlimited plan, you have five Guest seats from the get-go and will receive two additional guest seats for every Full Member you add to your workspace.

- On the Business plan, you receive 10 Guest seats right away, and every additional Full Member on your workspace adds an additional five Guest seats.

Neither Full member nor Guest seats are person or email based. When one of your team members leaves, their seat opens up and is available for you to assign someone else to that seat for the period it has been paid for.

For example, if you paid for Johnny to be a Full Member of your workspace for the whole year, and he leaves after three months, you get a Full Member seat available. You can reassign this to someone for 9 months at no additional cost.

Understanding all the terminology around seats, such as guest, full member, free, and paid, can be quite confusing. So, to simplify, I've created a ClickUp cost estimator as part of the book bonuses, accessible here: https://askyvi.tips/SPMCBonus

This calculator precisely determines the remaining Guest seats based on your Full Members and plan. By using this estimator, you will also be able to tell how many Full Members you need to add when or if you ever run out of Guest Seats.

Now that we've covered the user, let's look at the pricing of plans and how you can upgrade or downgrade your plan.

Plans and pricing

The easiest way to check current ClickUp pricing is by going to their pricing page at ClickUp.com/pricing. There you'll find a complete comparison of the features in each plan.

If you get overwhelmed trying to estimate what your cost is going to be for your setup, don't worry! Simply refer to my cost estimator which you can find within the book bonuses at: https://askyvi.tips/SPMCBonus – it will tell you exactly what your investment is going to be. It might help you save more money, all while making the most of your ClickUp account!

Now, upgrading your ClickUp workspace is really easy; just follow these steps:

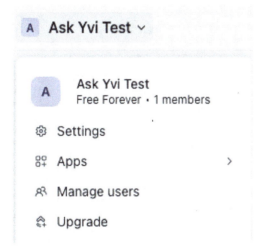

1. Go into your workspace icon in the top left and open your account menu. There you will either find an Upgrade button as pictured in *Figure 1.1.*

Or click the Settings menu item to find the Billings tab in your workspace settings.

Figure 1.1 – Upgrade Your FREE ClickUp Workspace

2. In the billing tab, you will see the different plans, such as:

- **Unlimited**: Perfect for personal use or to try out ClickUp
- **Business**: Great for solopreneurs or small teams
- **Business Plus:** For bigger teams, serious content creators
- **Enterprise:** For companies wanting white labeling, serious permission control, or have corporate-specific needs

Tip:

I usually recommend getting the Business Plus plan and using my coupon code you can find in the book bonuses right here: https://askyvi.tips/SPMCBonus because it will allow you to use all the features without any limitations.

3. Next, choose if you'd like to pay Yearly or Monthly and click on the Upgrade button:

Figure 1.2 – ClickUp Billing

4. Choose if you'd like to add ClickUp AI *(or add it later)*.

5. Enter your payment details or check existing payment details.

6. Check your pricing and enter the promo code, which you can find in the Cost Estimator in the book bonus, by clicking *Enter Promo Code* in the cost section.

7. Now click the Upgrade button.

You are all set! Next, you'll see the Order Summary similar to the one displayed in the following figure:

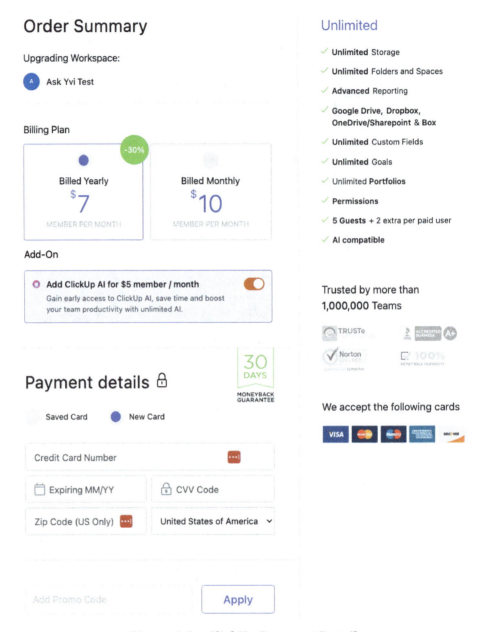

Order Summary

Upgrading Workspace:

🅰 Ask Yvi Test

Billing Plan

Billed Yearly	Billed Monthly
-30%	
$7	$10
MEMBER PER MONTH	MEMBER PER MONTH

Add-On

⬡ **Add ClickUp AI for $5 member / month**
Gain early access to ClickUp AI, save time and boost
your team productivity with unlimited AI.

Payment details 🔒

30 DAYS
MONEYBACK
GUARANTEE

○ Saved Card   ● New Card

Credit Card Number   •••

📅 Expiring MM/YY   🔒 CVV Code

Zip Code (US Only) •••   United States of America ▾

Add Promo Code   **Apply**

Unlimited

✓ **Unlimited** Storage
✓ **Unlimited** Folders and Spaces
✓ **Advanced** Reporting
✓ **Google Drive, Dropbox, OneDrive/Sharepoint & Box**
✓ **Unlimited** Custom Fields
✓ **Unlimited** Goals
✓ Unlimited **Portfolios**
✓ **Permissions**
✓ **5 Guests** + 2 extra per paid user
✓ **AI compatible**

Trusted by more than
1,000,000 Teams

TRUSTe   ACCREDITED BUSINESS A+
Norton SECURED   100% MONEYBACK GUARANTEE

We accept the following cards

VISA MasterCard Maestro AMERICAN EXPRESS DISCOVER

Figure 1.3 – ClickUp Payment Details

Now that you have set up your ClickUp account it's time to start digging into the ClickUp hierarchy, how it's structured, and what that means for your projects within ClickUp.

The ClickUp Hierarchy

As you might have already gathered, your account with ClickUp - your business setup - is called a **Workspace**. Think of your workspace as your business as a whole. It houses everything – your internal departments, training, and resources – you can even add your personal tasks.

> **Tip:**
>
> Don't just think of ClickUp as your work only project management tool! Simply add a private space in your ClickUp workspace and set it to be private for your eyes only. This approach is so much easier than getting (and potentially paying for) a second workspace just to handle your private tasks and projects.

Which brings us to the second layer in the ClickUp hierarchy, **Spaces**.

Think of ClickUp Spaces as your overlaying collection of everything pertaining to a topic in your business. Spaces are often used in conjunction with your internal business departments, such as:

- Admin
- Client or Product Delivery
- HR or Team Training
- Content Creation
- Growth
- Operations

Right below Spaces, there are Folders.

Folders allow you to house a collection of Lists. When you have a Space for your client delivery, for example, your Folder would be the client you are working with, the Lists below the services rendered, as well as some other potential supporting Lists. Supporting Lists could be onboarding or client assets - you will find more about this specific example in *Chapter 4, ClickUp Best Practices*.

Just like Folders can house multiple Lists, a List can house - you guessed it - all your **Tasks**. And the fun just keeps going! Within those Tasks, you can also have **Subtasks** and **Nested Subtasks**.

Figure 1.4 will help you visualize how all this works:

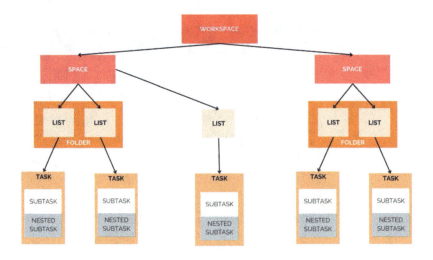

Figure 1.4 – ClickUp Hierarchy Layout

Within this hierarchy, there is one overlaying location; think of it as the master space. It is a view in ClickUp that is always there for every Full Member – it's called Everything view.

The Everything view shows you, as the name says, everything in your workspace. ALL OF IT.

Important Note:

The Everything view is only available to Full members because of how ClickUp handles users and sharing. Guests do not have an Everything view because Guests can only be invited to Folders and don't have access to ClickUp Spaces. You'll learn more about this in *Chapters 3 and 4* of this book, where we dive deeper into how you can work with your team and clients in ClickUp.

Figure 1.5 shows how ClickUp's hierarchy looks like within the ClickUp browser app:

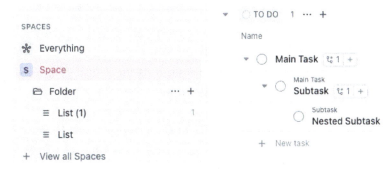

Figure 1.5 – The Hierarchy Within ClickUp

Now that you have already heard about the Everything view let's dive into ClickUp Views that you can set up yourself. But first, let's understand what are ClickUp Views and why they're so important.

What are ClickUp Views?

Views in ClickUp allow you to visualize your project at hand in different visual layouts. Views in ClickUp is probably one of my favorite features. ClickUp views allow you to show the same data in different layouts.

The most common views you probably already know are List View, your Checklist-type View, and Kanban or Board View as it is called in ClickUp.

These allow us to show our tasks in a to-do list type layout if you or your team are Type-A kind of people, and at the same time, you can add a second view showing the exact same tasks in a Kanban-style board view, often preferred by artistic humans, or a more timeline-focused Gantt chart view for your team member who keeps everyone on track.

There are many more views in ClickUp, some of which even give you more functionality than just task management.

Shall we take a look at the two categories of views in ClickUp?

Task views allow you to display your tasks in different layouts. Whereas custom Page views allow you to add even more additional information and features to your project and tasks.

- **Task view**: Task Views allow you to see your task information on a List, Board, or Calendar view. You can also observe their connectivity in the Gantt view and examine how work is divided among team members in the Box view.

- **Page view**: Page views allow you to add additional resources alongside your tasks. Add Documents, use the Whiteboard View, or even embed other tools.

You can add both of these categories of views at:

- Everything view level
- Space level
- Folder level
- List level

Choose the location of your view based on your needs and click + View in the upper view menu.

Then follow these steps to create a view:

1. Choose the view you'd like to add.
2. Name your view all the way on top of the menu.

3. Choose if you'd like this to be a Private view – if you want to pin it, click on Pin view.
4. And lastly, click the Add button to generate your view.

Figure 1.6 will show you where to find all these different custom views in your ClickUp:

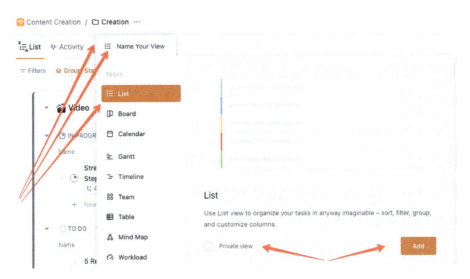

Figure 1.6 – Add View In ClickUp

Now, let's take a look at what specific views are available and how you can use them.

Task views in ClickUp

You now know what views in ClickUp are and how to add them, let's take a closer look at the different kinds of Task Views available to you.

*   **List**: This is the most popular approach to keeping track of and prioritizing your activities. In ClickUp, the list view is a necessary task view that must be used for each Space, Folder, and List. It's the most adaptable viewpoint in terms of clustering, sorting, and filtering tasks.

- **Board**: This is the favorite of kanban fans. It shows you tasks in a pipeline and allows for easy drag-and-drop, making it simpler to move things about.

- **Calendar**: This is where you'll want to go for planning, scheduling, and managing resources. As you'd expect, in this view, all of your tasks are organized by their dates.

- **Gantt**: This view allows you to see how your tasks and subtasks are connected. It also lets you see which tasks are dependent on what set of tasks.

- **Timeline**: This view allows you to visualize your project schedule and easily see your full project roadmap, plan timelines, and manage resources.

- **Team**: It gives you insight into what people are working on, what they have done, and who has open resources or has way too many tasks. This is perfect for project managers to keep their team on track.

- **Table**: Think of this view as your spreadsheet view.

- **Mind Map**: You can visually lay out your workspace hierarchy or create your free-form Mind Map to plan and organize projects, ideas, or anything you can imagine.

- **Workload**: This is your view to visualize your team's capacity and manage resources. Quickly see who got too much on their plate and whose time is not fully utilized.

- **Activity**: Ever wonder what's happening in your workspace? This view allows you to see what activity is going on in a list, folder, or space.

- **Map**: It shows you the locations of your tasks. It utilizes the location Custom Field to pull the location data.

Up next are the Page Views.

Page Views in ClickUp

I know that was quite a lot of task views, but stay with me, we're not done yet. Next, let's explore the ClickUp page views available to you along with their use cases:

- **Whiteboard**: These are collaborative work areas you can add at the Everything, Space, Folder, or List level as views.
- **Doc**: It enables you to create and collaborate in ClickUp documents. Write meeting notes, Standard Operating Procedures, Wikis, and more.
- **Chat**: It does just what it says it does; it gives you the capability to add a chat wherever you'd like.
- **Embed**: This View allows you to embed anything you'd like, as long as it gives you the embed code. Google products and Figma can even be embedded with their share link - no embed code needed.
- **Form View**: Build forms in ClickUp that turn submissions automatically into tasks. Form Views are always associated with one List only.

You will see more of these views throughout this book when I give insights about specific use cases. We'll go over how all these views allow you to give yourself and your team everything you need to run your projects efficiently.

NOTE: *Some of these views have different limitations based on your plan, please refer to ClickUp's full feature list: https://clickup.com/pricing*

Now that you have a good understanding of the ClickUp hierarchy and its implementation, you can start structuring your own workspace. Use the concepts of Spaces, Folders, Lists, and Tasks to organize projects in a way that fits your needs.

While it may seem complex at first, the hierarchy is actually very flexible and enables extensive customization.

Speaking of customization, let's dive deeper into Tasks and how you can customize them to your needs and wishes!

Tasks 101

ClickUp tasks can have as much or as little information as you'd like. There are a few areas that will house different types of information. You have your general description area but also Custom Fields.

Why don't we take a look at all the different parts within a ClickUp task?

A Task in ClickUp has four parts, as you can see in the following images.

Upper Row: Think of this as your control room for your task. From left to right it entails navigation arrows to the previous or next task, the task location, the creation date of the task, your share button, task settings menu, favorite your task, move it into the task tray, your task layout (default, full screen, or sidebar) and the close button.

Figure 1.7 – ClickUp Task location

Important Note:

Check out the three different ways to show your task by changing the task layout!

Default: pop-up style task box
Full Screen: as the name says, takes over your full screen

Upper left task side: Is like the control board of your task. This is where you'll find your task ID, due date, task priority, time tracking and estimation, sprint points, tags, task cover image, status, assignees, task title and last but not least the task description area.

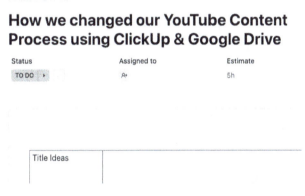

Figure 1.8 – Task Info

Lower Left Task Side: Houses additional assets and information for your task. This is where you will find your Custom Fields which we discuss in *Chapter 6.*

Right below that are the assigned comments from the activity view (*which we'll talk about in a second*), checklist(s), and any attachments.

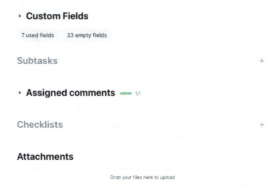

Custom Fields

7 used fields   33 empty fields

Subtasks   +

› **Assigned comments** ━ 1/1

Checklists   +

Attachments

Drop your files here to upload

Figure 1.9 – Task Additional Assets

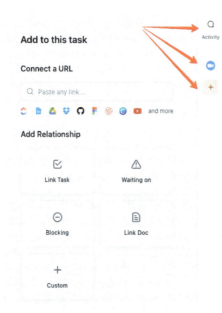

Add to this task

Connect a URL

🔍 Paste any link...

C B ▲ ⚡ ○ F ⊚ G ▶ and more

Add Relationship

☑   ⚠
Link Task   Waiting on

⊖   📄
Blocking   Link Doc

+
Custom

Right side activity view: Shows your task activity, let's you easily use any of your integrations like zoom, as well as manage dependencies, and link other tasks or docs.

Figure 1.10 – Task Activity

Putting it all together gives you your task list and all the information associated with it. In *Figure 1.11*, you can see how all of this comes together in an active task:

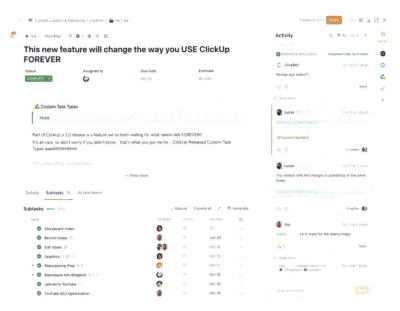

Figure 1.11 – Task With Details

Once you get more active in your tasks, you will see subtasks, checklists, relationships, and attachments added to the task on the left side.

The right side will show you task activity, as well as emails sent from within these tasks, as well as comments posted. More on this to come throughout the book, as we dive deeper into Custom Fields and other activities within a task.

Summary

Throughout this book, you'll encounter more references to this chapter as we uncover more concepts and implement everyday use cases. A solid grasp of the content covered in this chapter will facilitate a clearer understanding of the material ahead.

In the next chapter, you will discover how to personalize your ClickUp workspace. This includes a deeper exploration of navigating ClickUp, customizing your notifications, and learning task management tricks to enhance your efficiency and productivity.

CHAPTER 2
Add Your Personalized Settings

The previous chapter provided a glimpse into the features and functionality available in ClickUp. This chapter focuses on personalizing ClickUp to suit your needs, covering everything from highlight colors in your Workspace to managing notifications effectively.

Pay close attention, as this chapter addresses common struggles beginners encounter, providing easy-to-implement best practices. You will learn some easy-to-implement best practices that will help personalize your ClickUp to allow you to be your most productive self.

This chapter covers:

- Personalizing your Workspace setting
- Changing your account settings
- Personalizing your notifications
- Configuring your Spaces and Lists settings
- Customized task settings
- Best practices of connecting ClickUp to your Google Calendar

By the chapter's end, your ClickUp Workspace will be personalized to suit your preferences, with customized colors, settings, and notifications to enhance your productivity.

Account and workspace settings

In ClickUp, we have two different settings when it comes to your Workspace. There are settings that impact the Workspace as a whole as well as your personal account settings.

You can find your company settings by clicking on your workspace avatar in the top left of your sidebar as shown in the *Figure 2.1*:

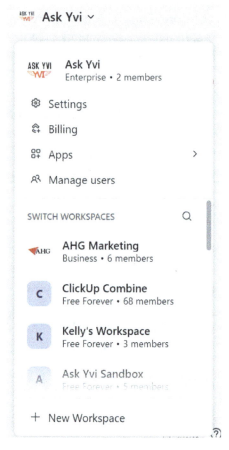

Figure 2.1 – ClickUp Settings

Pro Tip:

Use the same email address to join ClickUp Workspaces! Using the same email allows you to have all ClickUp Workspaces you are a member of as a list like this and easily switch between them.

Having all your ClickUp Workspaces connected to one email, and therefore all in one list, will also allow you to easily see if you have notifications in any of your Workspaces with a red dot displayed over the Workspace icon the notification is in.

The following screenshot shows such a notification dot:

Figure 2.2 – ClickUp Workspace Notification

ClickUp Workspace Settings

Once you click on Settings in your Workspace menu you will get quick access to the most used settings and features such as:

- **Settings**: Here you can change your logo, Workspace name, transfer your Workspace, or white label it. White labeling is an Enterprise feature and allows you to take off the ClickUp branding.
- **Import/Export**: Allows you to import tasks and projects into or out of ClickUp.
- **People**: Allows you to invite new Workspace members or guests.
- **ClickApps**: Allows you to add additional features to ClickUp. More on that in Chapter 3, Unlocking Additional Features with ClickApps.
- **Spaces**: Provides an overview of all Spaces within your Workspace and their details like statuses and ClickApps used within each Space.

- **Integrations**: Shows other tools that you have linked with your ClickUp.
- **Template Center**: Houses all of your personal as well as ClickUp's template library.
- **Trash**: Deleted something and didn't mean to? You might find it here.
- **Billing**: Allows you to upgrade/downgrade your Workspace or change your billing.
- **Security & Permissions**: This is where you turn on two-factor authentication, single sign-on, and manage your advanced user permissions.

Now that you have a great overview of all the Workspace settings and how to find them, let's look a little closer at some of the most important ones.

The People settings allow you to see which of the people in your Workspace are Members and who are Guests, as seen in *Figure 2.3*:

Figure 2.3 – Manage People

With the click of a button, you can change their access level or remove them completely from your Workspace.

When switching over from your Full members to the Guests tab, you'll additionally find information about what folders, lists, and tasks that guests have access to. You will also see what permissions they have within your Workspace as you can see in *Figure 2.4*.

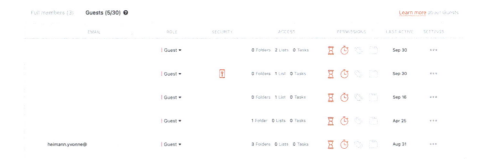

Figure 2.4 – ClickUp Guest Settings

> **Note:**
>
> Folders, lists, and tasks that guests have access to, are not shown in the Full members tab as these members have access to every public Space in your Workspace.

The other important option to mention in your settings is ClickApps.

If you ever find yourself saying: "*But I don't have that functionality in my ClickUp Workspace!*" Chances are - it's a functionality added through a ClickApp and it hasn't been turned on!

As you can see in *Figure 2.5*, there are quite a few ClickApps to choose from:

Figure 2.5 - ClickApps

Many of these ClickApps enable features in your ClickUp Workspace. Some of these features are enabled Workspace-wide, while for the rest, you need to choose which Spaces within your Workspace they get activated. Make sure you don't skip Chapter 3 as we'll be taking a closer look at all the ClickApps available to you.

Now that you know about your Workspace settings, let's take a look at your account settings in ClickUp.

ClickUp Account Settings

You can find your personal account settings in the top right of the ClickUp page. Simply click on your profile picture and as you can see in the image below, it opens up a menu that houses multiple items:

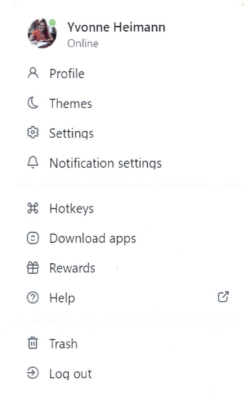

Figure 2.6 - ClickUp Personal Settings

Here's a brief of these items:

- **Profile**: It shows a summarized version of all your tasks and your calendar.

- **Themes:** Instead of just the dark mode, you can have your ClickUp any of the available colors.

- **Settings:** Includes your personal info, email, as well as your desired color theme, language, and date format.

- **Notification settings:** Allows you to determine which notifications you would like to get in your email, mobile app, web app, or in the browser app.

- **Hotkeys:** Gives a quick view of all hotkeys available to you within ClickUp.

- **Download Apps:** Will bring you to a new window where you will see every device and browser you can download ClickUp on.

- **Rewards:** Shows information related to ClickUp's referral program.

- **Help:** Opens the Help menu with additional resources.

- **Trash:** Your recently deleted things go here.

- **Log out:** As the name says, to log out of your account.

One of the most important settings within your ClickUp is your notification settings. ClickUp has granular capabilities that allow you to choose which notifications you'd like to receive in which app. Making sure you go into these settings and adjust them to your liking early on, will help avoid distractions and overwhelm from having way too many dings and rings every day.

With that settled, let's go over the key functions of the notification settings and how to customize them!

Personalize your notifications

Your Notification settings play a crucial role in determining how and where you receive notifications for changes in ClickUp. ClickUp's notification system is highly detailed, so let's explore the various ways you can receive notifications.

As mentioned in the previous section, accessing your notifications is easiest through the Settings menu on the bottom left. Once you enter your Notification settings, you will see the following options (*Figure 2.7*):

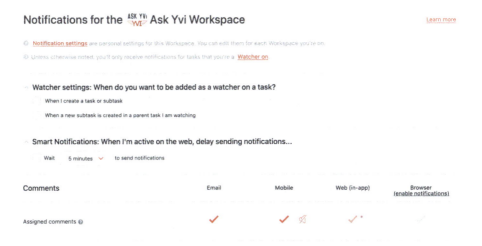

Figure 2.7 - ClickUp Notification Settings

The first setting you will see is the Watcher settings.

A watcher in ClickUp follows the process of a task just like an assignee would, without being assigned to any task. However, that also means you get notified like an assignee about anything that is happening, updated, or checked off in a task if your notifications are set accordingly.

This single checkbox can decide your notification sanity!

Ask yourself: "Do I need to watch and get notified about everything happening even though I'm not an assignee?" The answer is usually *NO*, but you do have the option to add yourself as a watcher for single tasks. This setting right here is a simple way to automatically monitor every task you create.

Pro Tip

Unchecking both Watcher settings, particularly Custom Views (which will be covered in Chapter 7), lets you keep an eye on activities with fewer interruptions. You can customize your notifications in a way that suits you and your team, enabling you to track progress on tasks and projects without being constantly dinged with updates.

Below the Watcher settings, you'll find Smart Notifications. This feature allows you to delay notifications while actively working in ClickUp.

Now that we've covered those, let's explore your Notification locations based on the app you're using:

- **Email:** These are emails sent to your Workspace email address.

- **Mobile**: These refer to your Android or iPhone.

- **Web (in-app):** These are notifications happening within ClickUp itself when you are using the browser application. Notifications that show up in your ClickUp notification tab. This is the reason why you will see some * on some of those and won't be able to turn them off. The * marked settings are required for ClickUp to work properly.

- **Browser:** These are notifications that your browser sends you directly. Have you ever seen those pop-up notifications where your browser told you about your next appointment? Or maybe a Slack update? Those are browser notifications, and you can set them up for ClickUp too.

Scrolling down the list of Notifications you will find a lot of different types of notifications based on ClickUp features, such as:

- **Comments**: These are any comments that are assigned to you or to other members, new comments, or any reactions in the comments.

- **Tasks**: These are changes in the tasks that are assigned, such as new tasks, status changes, and task name changes.

- **Start & Due Dates**: These remind us of any due date changes, due dates that are overdue, and other changes in the start date.

- **ClickApps**: The priority changes, adding and removing of tags, time tracking and estimates, and ClickBot notifications are seen here.

- **Integrations**: These notify if GitHub, GitLab, and Bitbucket are added.

- **List Info**: Notifications for changes in a list.

- **Doc and Chat Views**: These are comments that are assigned to you, or you are mentioned in, new comments, or any reactions outside the tasks.

- **Home**: This is where you can set your reminders.

- **Sharing**: These are the tasks, lists, folders, and docs, that are shared to you.

- **Docs**: Any pages that you are mentioned in.

Notification Recommendations:

You will learn ClickUp best practices in *Chapter 4* once you have a better understanding of the basics, but even before we get to that here's a ClickUp life hack you need to know: it's totally okay to turn off most of the notifications.

- For **ClickUp emails notifications**, it's best to turn everything off save for the Daily Due Dates summary email. Set the time on this email just before you usually start working. This way you have an email waiting for you every morning that shows you exactly what you need to get done that day.

- For the **ClickUp mobile app**, you can handle those notifications like you would a chat app. The only Notifications to keep on would be @ mentions of any kind and potentially when you are getting assigned. I also recommend having Reminders turned on for mobile as well as Priority change and Past Due. This recommendation is based on me working a lot on my mobile phone – it's my notification hub.

- When choosing your **Web (in-app) Notifications**, think of it as: *What do I need to know about the work happening in ClickUp to not miss anything while still being productive?* What do you want to see in your ClickUp Notification feed? For me, other than the ones you can't turn off, it is things like Priority changing, comments, reactions, as well as things getting shared with me.

- I also have **Browser Notifications** turned off, as I find them to be a bit overwhelming, and ClickUp is already handling all the notifications anyway. So, you probably will not need any Browser Notifications at all, just stay in ClickUp.

Notification Settings are some of the most involved settings within ClickUp. Now that you mastered those, things are getting a little less intense. How about we take a look at ClickUp's Space and List Settings next!

Space, Folder, and List settings

Space, Folder, and List settings in ClickUp all work quite similarly. These settings allow you to customize your Workspace as well as choose what ClickApps, and therefore features, are available.

There is quite a bit happening here, so let's start with Space settings.

You will find each of these settings by hovering over your Space, Folder, or list name in ClickUp and clicking the three dots that appear on the right of the name.

The menu will open up and you will see the following:

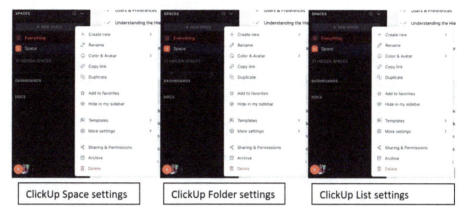

| ClickUp Space settings | ClickUp Folder settings | ClickUp List settings |

Figure 2.8 - ClickUp Space, Folder, And List Settings

As you can see in the preceding screenshot, many of the menu items are the same. And each of those menu items does the same thing, however, it changes the settings for the hierarchy item you opened the menu for.

Clicking Rename on Folder level will rename your folder. And clicking Copy link on Space level will copy the link for the whole Space.

Keep that in mind while we go through the menu items:

- **Create new:** Allows you to create a new Folder, List, or Custom View. It also allows you to generate from a template or Import.

- **Color & Avatar:** Allows you to update and change your Space color & icon.

- **Rename:** Let's you rename that Space, Folder, or List.

- **Copy link:** Copies the link to that location.

- **Duplicate:** Duplicates that location. This means if you duplicate a Space, it duplicates that Space and everything in it including all folders, lists, and tasks if you want.

- **Add to favorites:** Marks that location as a favorite and adds it to your Favorites menu.

- **Hide in my sidebar:** Moves the location out of your regular menu into the Hidden Spaces section at the bottom of your Spaces.

- **Templates:** Allows you to Browse, Save, or Update existing templates.

- **More settings** in:

  o **Space** - houses all your Space settings, Automations, ClickApps, Custom Task Fields and IDs, as well as Task statuses, and your Sort items on Space level.

  o **Folder** - has all your Automations, ClickApps, List statuses, and Sorting of your Lists.

  o **List** - here you'll find Automations, Custom Fields, and Lists status on List level.

- **Sharing & Permissions:** Allows you to set the location and all that's in it to Public or Private. Once you set it to private, you can start inviting Workspace members in this setting.

- **Archive:** Archives that location and all that's in it. This allows you to restore it again later.

- **Delete:** As the name says deletes that location and everything in it. If you delete a Space, it will delete the Folders and Lists in it too!

Pro Tip:

If you're unsure, always opt to Archive rather than Delete. If you archive something in ClickUp you can always bring it back. If you delete it then it goes to the trash, but Trash gets emptied after a certain amount of time, so it's likely that you won't be able to get it back.

Okay, that's a lot of settings. We have one more left. Are you ready to dive into your Task settings? I am! I guess I'll take you along no matter what! ;)

Task settings

Before we take a closer look at all things ClickUp Task Settings, remember when we talked about the Watcher setting in your Notifications?! If you need a little refresher, you can find that section in *Chapter 2*.

What I mentioned in that section is how you have the possibility to add Watchers later on. Look at *Figure 2.9*. Do you see the orange bell on the top right? That is where you can add or take off Watchers on each task and the number, in this case 1, indicates how many Watchers are on this task.

To add or remove a Watcher, simply click the bell and select or deselect team members.

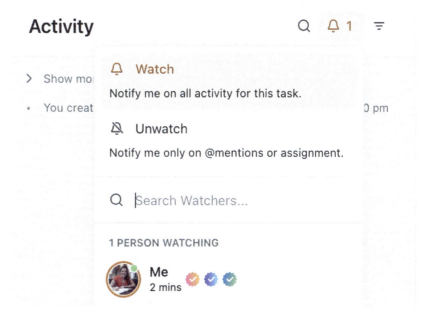

Figure 2.9 - ClickUp Watcher Settings

Now back to the main reason for this section, Task settings. You can find your ClickUp Task Settings by clicking the three dots in the top right. It is between the share button and the favorites, as you can see in the *Figure 2.10*:

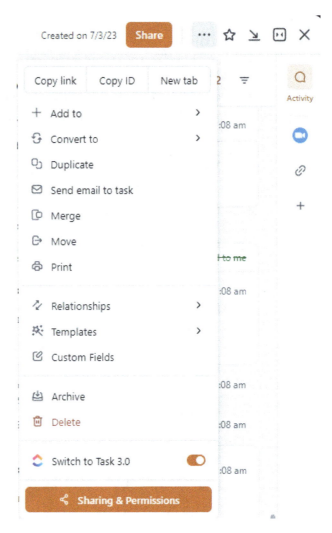

Figure 2.10 - ClickUp Task Settings

The first thing you'll see in the menu are three buttons that when clicked will:

- Copy the link to this task
- Copy the Task ID
- Opens this Task in a New Tab

After that row of buttons, you'll see your Task menu. Some of those menu items might look familiar to you from when we talked about Space, Folder, and List settings.

Let's get into the menu items and what it's for:

- **Add To:** Allows you to add the Task to another List, your favorites, to LineUp, or your ClickUp Tray.

- **Convert to:** Changes your task level to subtask or up to main task. You can also mark this task as a Milestone.

- **Duplicate:** Copies the task based on your specifications.

- **Send email to task:** Gives you an email address that allows you to send emails directly to this task which will be turned into a comment.

- **Merge:** Allows you to merge this task with another task.

- **Move:** Moves this task to a different location.

- **Print:** Prints your task.

- **Relationships:** Houses the relationships and allows you to create relationships to another task, dependency on or to another task, or documents.

- **Template Center:** Let's you browse, save, or update existing Templates.

- **Sharing & Permissions:** Opens the Sharing menu which shows you who has access to this task, gives you the Task Sharing links, as well as lets you set the task Private or Public.

- **Archive:** Helps archive the task.

- **Delete:** Deletes the task.

Sometimes though, you need to change things not only on a single task but on a series of tasks. Am I right? No worries, I got you covered in the next section.

Changing multiple tasks

Updating and changing multiple tasks in ClickUp is quite simple once you figure out how to make the Multi Toolbar show up.

Here's how to do it:

1. In List view, hover over a task to reveal the select button.
2. Select all the tasks you want to edit.
3. The Multi Toolbar will show up on top of your ClickUp.

Figure 2.11 shows you exactly where the select button and Multi Toolbar are located:

Figure 2.11 - ClickUp Task Multi Toolbar

ClickUp's Multi Toolbar allows you to edit the following on your tasks:

- Watcher
- Assignee
- Status
- Tags
- Convert Task to Subtask
- Move Tasks or add to multiple Lists
- Due Date
- Priority
- Milestone
- Dependencies
- Merge Tasks
- Link Tasks
- Set Custom Fields
- Archive
- Delete

And if you look at the right side of the Multi Toolbar, you'll see that you can even copy all the selected tasks to your clipboard. Right next to that, you will find a field that allows you to use ClickUp's /Slash Commands rather than the menu buttons.

Best practices to connect your Google Calendar

Many of us live our lives based on appointments and entries on our Google calendar, so it should be no surprise to you that ClickUp seamlessly integrates with GCal.

You can easily two-way sync your Google Calendar to ClickUp - allowing you to see both your ClickUp tasks in Google Calendar along with your Gcal appointments inside ClickUp. This way, you can get the best of both worlds!

However, syncing your ClickUp and GCal may result in things getting mixed up and overwhelming, so before you integrate the two apps, make sure you pay close attention to the best practices mentioned in this section!

First things first, let's look at how you can connect your Google Calendar with ClickUp, and sync your information from one app to the other.

To connect your Google Calendar to your ClickUp Workspace, go to My Settings as you've already done early in this chapter:

1. Click on your profile avatar on the top right.
2. Click on My Settings right below.

Once you are in your personal Settings, scroll down in the left menu and find Your Name | Calendar as you can see in *Figure 2.12*:

Figure 2.12 - Connecting Google Calendar

As you can see in the preceding image, Apple Calendar and Outlook calendar are also available. However, those are a one-way sync only. Meaning you can show your ClickUp tasks on those calendars. Those calendars won't show inside ClickUp.

If you're fine with that, simply click the Connect button and choose which tasks you'd like to one-way sync.

Once you hit Save, the subscription link will be generated for you as displayed in *Figure 2.13* which can be added to any calendar supporting iCal feeds.

Figure 2.13 - Connection Outlook or Apple

We are going to focus, however, on the 2-way sync with Google Calendar as it is quite the productivity hack, allowing you to make changes to tasks within Google calendar, and have those changes reflected in ClickUp too!

Click on the +Add Account and you will see the following:

Figure 2.14 - Sync ClickUp with Google Calendar

- **Sync events to ClickUp** will allow you to show your Google Calendar events within ClickUp.

- **Sync tasks to Google** will show your ClickUp task In Google Calendar.

Let's start with the easy one!

Here's how you sync your events to ClickUp

1. Click on the box that says: Sync events to ClickUp.
2. Click Next.
3. Sign into your Gmail account if necessary.
4. Select your Google account.
5. Click Next.

And you are done! It's really that easy.

Up next is where the real magic happens... syncing your tasks into Google Calendar:

1. Click on the box that says: Sync tasks to Google.
2. Click Next.
3. Sign into your Gmail account if necessary.
4. Select your Google account.
5. Click Next.

I always recommend syncing everything assigned to me as shown in *Figure 2.15*:

1. Pick the Google Calendar you want to sync your ClickUp tasks to.
2. Choose which ClickUp location you'd like to sync.
3. Choose if you'd like to sync your tasks only or All tasks.

Figure 2.15 - Sync Task into Your GCal

This ensures you always see all your scheduled tasks in your calendar.

Pro Tip and Best Practice

Set up a Google Calendar *solely* for your ClickUp tasks! This will be the GCal you sync your ClickUp tasks to. Just like I did in *Figure 2.17*. This will allow you to show or not show your tasks in ClickUp. It will also allow you to quickly delete your ClickUp tasks in Gcal if this sync ever goes crazy and does not work as planned. This trick has saved my clients and me many hours when tasks get mistakenly added!

Okay, I know this was a lot of the dry... *click here* ... *do that* ... settings stuff. But I promise the upcoming chapters will bring more fun since we will go through real-life use cases and how you can add to ClickUp's standard features. So, stay tuned!

Summary

And with that, you have all the fine details and settings covered. You've learned to manage your Notifications, make your Workspace look more on-brand, and adding your logo. You also got the hang of how Task settings work and the best way to use them. Great work!

Now, take a deep breath and maybe grab your drink of choice before we get to the next chapter and take an even closer look at ClickApps aka *the super cool and fancy features in ClickUp*.

CHAPTER 3

Unlocking Additional Features with ClickApps

By now you've been using ClickUp and have gotten somewhat familiar with its basic functionality. For further clarity, you can always check my YouTube channel (https://www.youtube.com/c/askyvi) to get more practical examples of what you are learning here.

While watching some of those videos, you might come across a feature or functionality that seemingly is not available in your Workspace... No worries! I promise your ClickUp is not broken.

Depending on your ClickUp plan, you probably have those features too. In this chapter, I will show you how to unlock these features and make your ClickUp even more powerful.

What we use to add and manage these features to your Workspace are called **ClickApps**.

In this chapter, we will be covering the following topics:

- What are ClickApps
- Beginner ClickApps
- Advanced ClickApps

Technical requirements

Some of these ClickApps that we'll be talking about are not available in the Free Forever plan and require one of the paid plans you've already read about in *Chapter 1*.

You don't have to worry about upgrading at this point in time! ClickUp has this cool thing that if you are trying to use a ClickApp that is not available in your plan, you will get notified with a warning or pop-up in ClickUp.

For the most part, you likely already have what you need available on there. It's better to focus on getting the hang of what's accessible to you first before you make the decision to upgrade your Workspace.

> **Pro Tip**
>
> When you are ready to upgrade, I highly recommend going with the Business or Business Plus plan. The cost is easily off-set by the time the additional features and capability saves you... and not to forget, you do get savings in the book bonuses too!!
>
> Don't forget to grab those at: https://askyvi.tips/SPMCBonus

What Are ClickApps

As I mentioned earlier, ClickApps are apps within ClickUp that add more specialized functions to your ClickUp Workspace.

Some of these ClickApps automatically apply to your Workspace as a whole, while others require you to choose to which Space within your Workspace you want it to be applied to.

To find all ClickApps available in your Workspace, go to the Settings menu at the top left of the main screen and click on Apps, then click on ClickApps, as you can see in *Figure 3.1*:

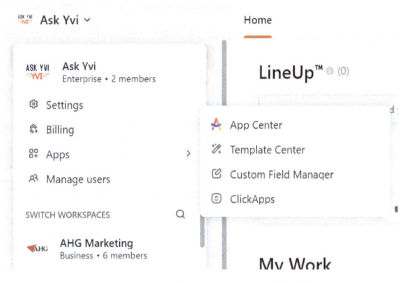

Figure 3.1 – Finding your ClickApps

Once you are in your ClickApps settings you will see two columns as displayed in *Figure 3.2*.

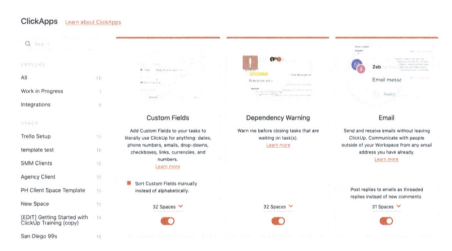

Figure 3.2 – ClickApps

In the left column, you will find a search box that allows you to search for specific ClickApps by name.

Below the search box, you will see two menus. The first one lets you explore your ClickApps while the second menu allows you to show ClickApps based on a single Space. Once you click on one of your Spaces listed there, you will only see the active ClickApps that are used in that Space.

In the right column, you will see all your ClickApps. The ClickApps shown there are all the ones available to you in your Workspace. However, if you make a selection in the menu on the left, you will see the active ClickApps based on your selection.

Let's take a look at the different settings you might see when enabling ClickApps.

As you can see in Figure 3.3, these settings can look a little bit different based on if the app is available all throughout your Workspace or if you need to decide which Workspace you'd like to add this app to.

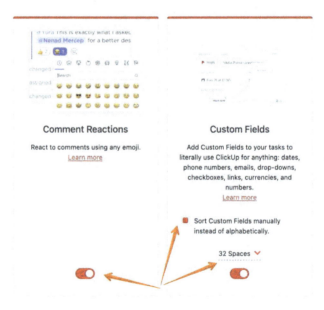

Figure 3.3 – Different ClickApps Settings

The ClickApp on the left called Comment Reactions, is an app that you enable for the whole Workspace. On or off are your only choices here.

Looking at Custom Fields on the right, you will see there are a few more options available.

First, you have your on/off switch you already know right at the bottom.

Then you get to choose if you'd like your Custom Fields sorted alphabetically or by clicking the checkbox to sort them manually.

And lastly, below the checkbox, you see your selection field to which Spaces you'd like to apply this ClickApp. Clicking the down arrow will open a list of all your Spaces. Now by clicking those Spaces you get to turn this functionality on or off, Space by Space.

It's time to take a closer look at what features these ClickApps add to your Workspace. There are a lot of them, so let's start with some of the frequently used ones.

Beginner ClickApps

In this section, we'll be taking a closer look at what I consider beginner ClickApps. These apps enable features that go alongside what someone just starting ClickUp would need and work with daily. They might also just simply add some fun to your Workspace.

The perfect ClickApps to start experiencing a more optimized ClickUp workspace are the following:

- **Clip: Screen Recording:** Think of it as your ClickUp version of Loom screen recording.

- **Collaborative Editing:** Allows you to edit tasks and Docs in ClickUp as well as see who is editing while they are editing.

- **Comment Reactions:** Who doesn't like emoji reactions? This option lets you add them to your comments.

- **Custom Fields:** We use ClickUp Custom fields in so many ways, so don't wait to activate them.

- **Dependency Warning**: Warns anyone trying to mark a task as done if the task is still in a dependency waiting for another task to be done.

- **Docs Home:** Enables a central location for all your ClickUp Docs.

- **Giphy:** Allows you to add Gifs in your comments, Docs, or descriptions to add a little flair.

- **Incomplete Warning:** Making sure you are really done even though there are still unresolved items in that task.

- **LineUp:** Turns on the LineUp feature in your ClickUp Workspace Home.

- **Multiple Assignees:** Allows you to add more than one assignee to tasks when turned on.

- **Preview Word, Excel, and PowerPoint files in ClickUp:** Don't just link your 365 files but also see a preview using this feature.

- **Priority:** Gives you colored flags to mark your tasks by level of importance.

- **Pulse:** Shows you in real-time who is online and what they are working on.

- **Quick-Create Statuses:** Allows you to quickly add Statuses by clicking between List view Status groups.

- **Remap Subtask Due Dates**: This is one of my most favorite features because it allows you to remap your Subtasks Due Dates automatically based on changing the main Task Due Date.

- **Tags:** Enables tags on your tasks.

- **Threaded Comments:** Just like in Slack, you can add a reply to a comment and rather than having this long string of comments, you can put them in threads.

- **Time Estimates:** This feature helps you plan your workload better.

- **Time Estimates Rollup:** Sums up the Time Estimates in your Subtask to one single number in your main task.

- **Time Tracking:** Turns on ClickUp's native time tracker.

- **Time Tracking Rollup:** Sums up all the subtasks' tracked time into one single number in your main task.

- **Who's Online:** Gives you a dot indicator right next to every ClickUp Members avatar that indicates if they are online or not.

- **Zoom:** Allows you start a Zoom meeting within ClickUp by using the meeting button or the slash command.

Next, let's see some best practices for these beginner ClickApps.

Best practices on using the beginner ClickApps

Clip: Screen Recording requires you to have the link handy or your recording will be forever lost in the black hole of the internet (*kind of like those socks that always seem to disappear in your clothes dryer*).

Unfortunately, there is no central location that houses all your recordings. It's best to save your video links somewhere secure, that way you can refer back to it when needed and you won't be forced to record the same thing all over again.

Dependency Warning, even though I don't recommend diving into Dependencies right away (*think: one task needs to be marked done for another task to become actionable*), but it would be good to turn this warning on early on.

The dependency warning automatically reminds your team to check if they can really mark this task closed or if there is a step that's not done yet.

Get used to using **Priority** early on to let your team know what needs to get done first, no matter the actual Due Date. We use this feature for our On Fire custom task list view that will be covered in *Chapter 10*. It will make priority management with your team a breeze.

Be careful while using **Quick-Create Statuses**! You should keep your Statuses in ClickUp limited and clean to not cause major issues in the future. Using a long list of different Statuses will make managing your team increasingly difficult. I dive more into the issue of Status vs Stages in this video: https://askyvi.tips/StatusVsStages.

With that in mind, just quickly creating a new Status on the fly can quickly turn into way too many statuses. Hence, I recommend keeping this ClickApp off.

Now that you have a good understanding of the basics of the ClickApps, let's dive into some of the more advanced features that ClickApps allow you to add to your ClickUp Workspace.

Advanced ClickApps

How about we get a little nerdier with our ClickUp features?

In this section, you will learn about how to take your project management to the next level using advanced ClickApps. We will go over how to specifically implement many of these in everyday use cases that I will be covering in later chapters.

At the end of this section, you will also find some best practices, giving you a fast track to lessons we learned over the years about using these ClickApps.

But first, let's look at what features are available to you through advanced ClickApps:

- **Automations**: Lets you automate a lot of things right in ClickUp.

- **Custom Task IDs:** This is a great feature when you want to use ClickUp as a support or ticketing tool as it lets you customize them and make them easier identifiable.

- **Dashboards:** Adds ClickUp Dashboards to your Workspace.

- **Default Private Views**: Defaults every new View to be set to private.

- **Email**: Turns on ClickUp's email feature and lets you email directly out of a task.

- **Milestones**: Enables you to mark milestones in your task process.

- **Nested Subtasks**: Allows you to add additional levels to your subtasks.

- **Not Started Status Group**: Adds a Not Yet Started grouping option to your Statuses.

- **Relationships**: Adds the capability of linking aka relationships of tasks, Docs, and more to your workspace.

- **Reschedule Dependencies**: If a *blocking* task's Due Date is changed, ClickUp will change the **Due Date** on the connected waiting on tasks accordingly.

- **Sprint Points**: Allows you to add point estimates to your sprints.

- **Sprints**: Enables the Sprint feature within ClickUp. Often used for agile project management.

- **Tasks in Multiple Lists**: Don't just have your tasks in one list. Add it to as many lists as you like.

- **Total time in Status**: Keep an eye on how long your tasks are hanging out in each Status.

- **Work in Progress Limits**: Lets you set soft limits in board view to better manage you and your team's workload.

Whew! You still here? Of course, you are! :D

Time to take a look at what all these ClickApps really mean and how they could be combined to achieve a specific outcome.

If you are working in an Agile Framework, you will need the Sprint Points, Sprints, and Tasks in Multiple Lists. These ClickApps will allow you to structure your ClickUp accordingly and run your sprint efficiently.

However, if you are trying to build more of a database-type Space in your ClickUp, like a CRM for example, Relationships is the ClickApp predominantly used to make that happen. The Relationship ClickApp allows you to link aka set up a relationship between tasks in different locations in ClickUp.

Work in Progress Limits and Total time in Status allows you to better manage your team and their workload.

As I mentioned before, many of these are different use cases and you will even find chapters in this book that focus specifically on ClickApps like Automations and Dashboards to help you get a deep understanding of their functionality.

Like we did in the previous section, let's look at some of the best practices for the advanced ClickApps.

Best practices on using the advanced ClickApps

It's important to slowly and intentionally ease yourself into ClickUp Automations. I've seen it many times where users get a little too excited to automate something they haven't even tested yet - resulting in creating more mess and confusion rather than helping simplify their processes.

I recommend getting comfortable with ClickUp's custom List views and filters first before going straight into Dashboards. Having a clear understanding of what's going on and what is possible in the Task Views will allow you to easily add even more magic to your ClickUp setup when you dive into Dashboards.

Nested Subtasks are amazing, I recommend not going more than three layers down. You don't want to truncate your workflow and process with so many levels that your team is either overwhelmed or confused when trying to switch from a big picture to a granular view. Keep the levels short and sweet – 3 layers, works best.

Tasks in Multiple Lists is another epic feature that works for so many different applications. Wherever the task is shared, everyone that has access to that location can see everything that is happening in that task.

The advanced ClickApps is often where a lot of the extra fanciness tends to hide in ClickUp. Don't worry! You will hear more about ClickApps all throughout this book as we go deeper into everyday use cases and how to implement those ClickApps features in your Workspace.

Summary

We've covered a lot of additional features available to you in ClickUp through ClickApps. Honestly, this can be overwhelming in the beginning, but once you get the hang of implementing one, the rest won't feel as complicated.

With all of these fun additional features, there are a lot of different ways to implement them. I think this is a perfect time for us to dive into some best practices in ClickUp, don't you think?

Join me in the next chapter as I share with you some common mistakes users make in ClickUp and the best practices to prevent that from happening to you.

CHAPTER 4

ClickUp Best Practices

ClickUp is an amazing project management tool with features that many other tools have fallen short of... but even with all those robust features, it can still possibly hurt your productivity, especially if you find yourself making the same mistakes new users end up doing.

Before you shake your fists at the heavens, let me share a word of advice. The truth is sometimes the reason we're doing it wrong is because we're unaware of what we don't know.

Over the years, after working with hundreds of clients, supporting community members, and using ClickUp myself, the list of best practices has grown bigger and bigger as I come across so many different ways to use ClickUp.

Ready to get ahead with your ClickUp game?

In this chapter, you will learn the best practices in ClickUp that will allow you to continuously grow and evolve in ClickUp minus the struggle of: *If only I'd known this sooner!*

We will cover the following main topics in this chapter:

- General Recommendation
- Status versus Stages
- Communication inside ClickUp
- Starting your day in ClickUp

Technical Requirements

To follow along and understand the details of this chapter, you need to know the basics of ClickUp Statuses, which is covered in *Chapter 2, Adding Your Personalized Settings*.

This chapter also covers ClickUp Custom Fields, so make sure you have read *Chapter 3, Unlocking Additional Features with ClickApps.*

General Best Practices

I said it before, and I'll say it again...

Keep it short and simple!

The first best practice I want to share with you is to keep your task descriptions short, simple, AND clear.

A good rule of thumb is that your task description should fit on one line in ClickUp. This ensures that you are describing the task at a high level without getting into too much detail.

If you find yourself writing a longer description, consider breaking the task down into smaller subtasks. This will help you stay focused on the individual steps required to complete the task, rather than getting lost in the details.

Use custom fields to add context

Custom fields are an amazing way to add context to your tasks in ClickUp. By default, every task has a few standard fields like Due date, Assignee, and Priority. However, you can add custom fields to any task to track additional information. You will learn more about the power of ClickUp Custom Fields in *Chapter 6: Setting Up and Using ClickUp Custom Fields.*

For this chapter, all you need to know right now is ClickUp's Dropdown Custom Field which allows you to add a Custom Field for single select type information. This field is what we use for the first best practice in ClickUp.

Status vs Stages

This is arguably the most important section in this book. I first brought up the topic of Status versus Stages in ClickUp, back in 2020 in one of my YouTube videos. The response was incredible with hundreds of comments and DMs. Even ClickUp team members started adjusting their internal setups.

Get this wrong and you'll find yourself fighting an uphill battle against an inefficient process. It is also the most time-intensive change if you want to update your ClickUp setup later on.

Let me explain...

Status versus Stages is the concept of understanding their differences and knowing when to appropriately use them in your Workspace. Statuses show you if someone is actively working on the task, whereas Stages tell you in which Stage of the Process your task is in.

Now you might say: ***"But Yvi, why can't I just use Statuses for that?!"***

ClickUp allows us to set up as many different statuses as we like. We get to name them and sort them as we please, including Not Started and Done Statuses. Oh, the possibilities!

And then one day, you are looking at your team's workload and you see a list of 10,000 different statuses - suddenly you realize you have no idea what your team is actually up to.

You have no idea if your team is actively working on tasks and which tasks they are working on. You might have set up your statuses using something like *video edit* because it's part of the process or *Monday* because you wanted to be able to plan your week in Board View by day of the week.

I love building custom views like the two examples above. And they are done quite simply in ClickUp. We just don't use Statuses for that.

So, let's start at the beginning.

What should Statuses in ClickUp look like for you to be able to tell at a glance what your or your team's workload looks like and still be able to build custom views that fit your need and workflow?!

Status

Statuses in ClickUp should always be activity based!

Think of the person doing the work. The actual task and the stages the task go through comes later (*see what I already hinted at there*?!)

For 95% of your ClickUp Spaces, you want to use the following Statuses in some variations:

- To Do
- In Progress
- Waiting Internal
- Waiting External
- Proof
- Done

As you can see in the image below, we chose Proof to be a Done status. You can keep it as an active status if you want to ensure whoever is proofing the work gets notified if the task is past due.

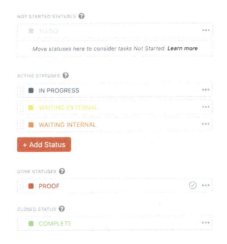

Figure 4.1 – ClickUp Standard Statuses

The goal here is to keep your Statuses as simple as possible.

We usually use four variations of this:

- Our standard status shown above
- One version with proof
- One without the proof status
- We also have a simple To Do status variation, which consists of:
  - *To Do*
  - *In Progress*
  - *Proof*
  - *Done*

Again, we use one version with the Proof Status and one without - based on if you need proofing for those tasks or not.

There are only a few use cases where we divert from this approach. Usually, those are cases where we use ClickUp as a database. I recommend using this even for CRM setups.

I know, I know... there are a lot of consultants out there saying differently, but let me ask you this: Does Onboarding tell you if someone is actively taking care of that client?? *NO*. It just means that the client is in the stage of onboarding. The Status *In Progress* and the assignee would tell you that someone is taking care of your client and who that client is.

This brings us to Stages...

Stages

Technically, Stages in ClickUp are a Dropdown Custom field.

I will always caution you to not go overboard and create thousands of Stages because *simplicity = productivity*.

I won't be as strict and limiting with Stages as I am with Statuses though, because stages allow you to do all the magic I mentioned in the beginning of this section.

You want a weekly board view? **Stages.**

You want to show the process your video goes through in production? **Stages.**

You want to know where that lead is in your sales process? **Stages.**

Let's take a closer look at how to use Stages on the example of a CRM in ClickUp, allowing you to manage your leads and sales funnel.

In *Figure 4.2* below, you will see the combination of the custom Dropdown Fields and how they would look like.

CLIENT STAGE	LEAD PROCESS	LEAD STAGES	LEAD SOURCE
Discovery Call	Service Recommendati...	Keep Warm	Referral
Discovery Call	no reply follow up (2nd)	Never replied	Other

Figure 4.2 – Result of Combined ClickUp Stages

This is the list of potential custom Dropdown Fields you might use.

Potential Client Stage:

- Discovery Call
- Active Client
- Offboarding
- Inactive Client
- Not a Client

Potential Lead Process Stages:

- Initial Email Send
- No Reply Follow-Up (2nd)
- Magic Email (3rd & last)
- Service Recommendation Send

Potential Lead Stages:

- Won
- Lost
- Keep Warm
- Not a Fit
- Needed Tech Help
- Spam
- Never Replied

The combination of those fields allows us to easily keep track of all we need to know about every lead that's coming through our process.

The Lead Process Stages allow me to know exactly where in our email process the lead is. The moment they scheduled a discovery call they start the client process, and in the future the Lead Process field will tell us how well we convert clients and how many emails it took us to get them on a discovery call. Whereas the Client Stage allows us to tell easily where we are at when working with a client.

And last but not least, the Lead Stage allows us to tell if we won a client, or if they actually should have just contacted ClickUp support. ;)

Now that you have a great understanding of the difference between Statuses and Stages in ClickUp, let's take a closer look at Status and their best practices.

Using due dates and assignees

Too often, I see users not set Due Dates or add Assignees to their tasks.

Before I dive into the whole psychological and productivity issue with skipping that step, let me ask you this...

So, you are going through this process of learning ClickUp. You might even already upgraded to a paid plan using my savings in the book bonus, but to do what? Use ClickUp as a glorified to-do list? Because that's what it is if you don't set Due Dates or assignees. Yes, even if the assignee is you!

I am assuming you chose ClickUp to be more productive. You probably own a business and might even want to add to your team and scale. That requires commitment, boundaries, and time management. You can't manage any of those without assigning your tasks and setting Due Dates.

Let's dive a little into the psychology of this.

It's human nature to give a task all the time it needs. Which means if you do not set a deadline, aka Due Date, there is a good chance most of those tasks will still be sitting in your ClickUp for months... untouched.

Those *No Due Date* tasks might be important, or they might not be important. You still need to sort through them, because there's bound to be a reason why you noted those down in the first place, right?

So, how do you easily find all the tasks without dues dates? Just follow these steps!

1. Go into your Everything View and go to your List View.
2. In that list View click the Group By button and choose Due Date as pictured below.

3. Notice the arrow beside the Due Date, click on it again so it points down.

All your No Due Date tasks are now on top of your list!

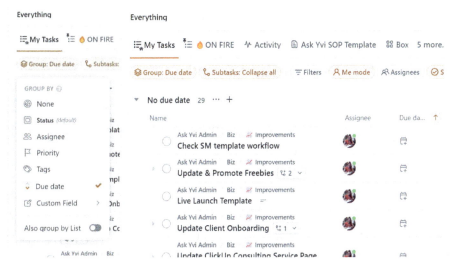

Figure 4.3 – Tasks with no Due Date

Now, it's your turn to go through these tasks.

We will talk about asset management later in this book and specifically how to filter out those ClickUp lists or folders in a Custom View in *Chapter 7*. For now, I'm assuming at this point in time you use ClickUp solely for task management. This means ALL these tasks *have to have due dates*. If you're a business owner, here's how you can tidy this up:

- **A task that is important now**: Set the due date and assign it to you or your executive assistant.

- **A task that is important later**: Set the due date at a later date and assign it to you or your executive assistant.

- **A task that is not important now**: Set a due date now and delegate it (*you should only focus on important tasks in your business*).

- **A task that is not important later**: You can delete it. Chances are this task has no importance and you will continuously push it out further and further. Be honest with yourself now and save yourself the headaches.

Now that we have your **Due Dates** cleaned up, there might still be some unassigned tasks left.

Let's double check...

Go back to your Group By field and change it to Assignee. Make sure the little arrow next to it is still pointing down. Just like pictured below. Now all your Unassigned tasks are on top of your list.

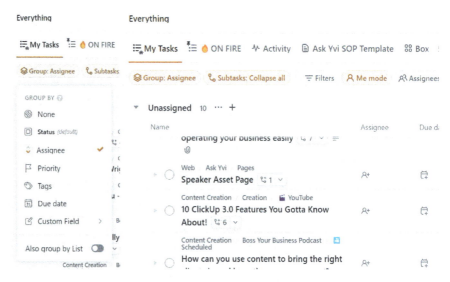

Figure 4.4 – Tasks with no Assignee

Once you get this all cleaned up, you can change your Group By back to Status and set your arrows to how you'd like your Status sorting to show up.

We will dive even deeper into custom views and all the magic that grouping and filtering brings to your custom views in *Chapter 7*, after we have covered all the fundamentals.

Communication inside ClickUp

Communication is a big topic in companies, and this doesn't apply only to ClickUp.

Unclear and disorganized communication is the biggest reason for missed deadlines and major profit loss. How can you ensure that you and your team do their best and create an environment that supports clear communication throughout everything you do?

You do so in 2 very actionable steps:

- Set clear communication guidelines
- Enforce those guidelines

Let's start with the basics: **Task conversations.**

Any conversation that is needed to get a task done should always happen on the task level. Keeping task-related communication in the comments section of the task you're working on allows every team member (or client) to see what has happened since work started. With this you can easily see changes and revisions in real time.

If something comes up during those task conversations and a new task evolves from a question, you can easily assign said comment. Hover over the comment for the Assign button to appear.

As you can see in the figures below that it also adds an Assigned to note within the comment as well as in the task management portion on the left column of your ClickUp task.

Figure 4.5 - Assigning Comments

No matter where in ClickUp the conversation is happening, don't forget to tag who you are talking to! You'll soon see why.

For overall project communication, I recommend adding a chat view on the list or folder level, based on how you use ClickUp's hierarchy for your projects. Meaning, if you follow my recommendation, for example: having a client space and each of your clients has their own folder:

- General client communication would be on the folder level
- Whereas service or department-specific chats would happen on the list level

But no worries! You will see more use case examples throughout the book when we dive into everyday practical examples.

Just remember for now: *Task communications always have to happen in the task and if someone wants something done, add a task, assign it, and set a due date.*

Now, how does one enforce these guidelines? **By reminding people.**

Picture this:

Your client is used to emailing everyone. So, they emailed you saying they would love to get this thing done.

You just added them to your ClickUp. This client had their introductory call where you explain to them how all this works... yet here they are – still emailing you.

It's really just a force of habit. Your client doesn't mean to be a pain and not listen to what you asked them to do. Their way of doing things has probably been the same for many years, and in this case, it's emailing people.

It is your job now to retrain that habit from emailing to adding a task. Simply tell your client: *Please add this to our To Do list in ClickUp.* Done. It's that easy. Same with your team.

It might take a few times of reminding them for this new habit to stick, but they will be thankful in the long run that nothing falls through the cracks anymore and things get done. And all of the above leads to our last best practice:

Starting your day in ClickUp

How you start your day in ClickUp impacts everyone on your team, including *you*.

The process I show you in this section has proved to be the most productive one. It allows your team, if you have one, to keep working on their tasks and sets you up for a predictive day yourself - knowing you won't miss anything.

This section is at the end of this chapter as all the above best practices support this last process. Meaning, the above best practices need to be followed for this process to work and to have the biggest impact.

Pro Tip

Set up a recurring task for yourself that includes the steps I mention below as subtasks. This will allow you to follow this best practice without ever having to think about it. ClickUp will tell you every morning what exactly you need to do.

I recommend you start your day in your Notifications:

1. Go to your left sidebar and click on Inbox.

2. This is where *Chapter 2* comes in quite handy - I hope you've cleaned up your notification settings by now. Or you will have a lot going on in your Inbox!

   You already did? Good, then you may proceed.

   You haven't yet? Please refer to *Chapter 2* and make sure you clean up your notifications settings first to make sure you don't get all the granular notifications *(it can be really distracting!)*.

OK. Everyone is ready? Let's do it!

In your Inbox go to Filter in the top right and click on @mentioning me like in *Figure 4.7* below:

Figure 4.7 – @ Mentions

As you can see, my amazing Head of Marketing, Kitty @mentioned me in a comment telling me one of our weekly email newsletters is ready for me to Proof.

In this case, I thanked her with an emoji and ***did not*** clear the notification by clicking the red arrow dot on the right. Why? Because tomorrow, when I'm back in the office, I'll go back to those notifications and make sure I go through and finalize all of the content she has ready for me.

Now if this was a question, I would either answer it right away so she can proceed with her work or if it requires an action of mine I would do so or create a task, assign it to me, and you guessed it, set a due date.

All of this happens following the best practice you learned earlier in this chapter!

For example:

- If I need to do something but can't do it right away, I need to set the task to Waiting Internally. Honestly, Kitty probably already finished that anyway ;) Once I'm done holding up the process, I change the status back to In Process and Kitty is notified that she can continue working on it or even wrap that task up.
- If we are waiting for a client or a subcontractor to do their thing, then we use the Waiting External status.

Once you reply to comments and answer questions you can move on to **Assigned to me** as you can see in the figure below:

Figure 4.8 – Assigned to Me

This is where you might discover some overdue tasks assigned to you. With a little bit of luck, you might have already taken care of it (*see the green box next to the task name? That means it's completed!*) and you can just click the red dot arrow on the right next to that notification and clear it.

If you clear this task overdue notification and it's not marked complete, it will pop up again tomorrow. You can also easily mark things complete if you've done them already or if no additional action needs to be taken. If that's the case, then just click the status box on the left of the task name and mark it complete.

Where these notifications become important for you and your team is the notification at the bottom of the image above. See how it says Assigned to me?

That means Kitty needs something from me. In this case, going over the email newsletter and leaving notes if I want to include an upcoming event or promotion. We have been working on growing our email list, so this assigned comment is important feedback she needs from me.

Now I know and I can go into the Google Document she so kindly linked for me, give her the answers she needs to continue the process, and I get to mark this assigned comment as Resolved by clicking the Resolve box on the bottom right of the notification.

And as I already mentioned above... All of this happens following the best practice you learned earlier in this chapter! Now that you took care of your @Mentions and Assigned to me it is time to check what's left:

1. Go to All in your Inbox as shown below:

Figure 4.9 – All Notifications

2. Once you take care of all that, it is time to schedule your day!

3. Go to your Home view by clicking on Home in your left sidebar.

4. Here you will find a collection of widgets that are customizable and can show you:

- **LineUp**
- **Calendar**
- **Agenda**
- **Recent**
- Assigned to me
- Reminders
- My Work

Take a look at *Figure 4.10* below to get familiar with this layout.

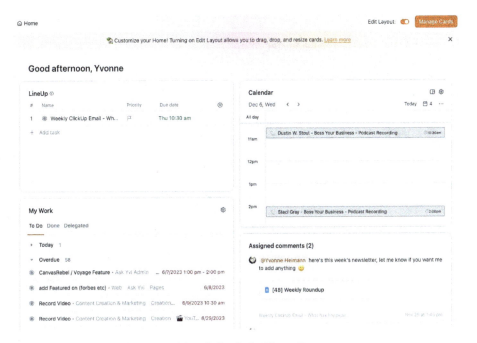

Figure 4.10 – Schedule Your Day page

Let's do some ClickUp housekeeping! In the calendar view on the right, if you have your Google calendar synced to your ClickUp, you still might not see your Google calendar events. To make sure you see the Google Calendar refer to *Figure 4.11* below. You can see how easy it is to choose which Google Calendars to display here.

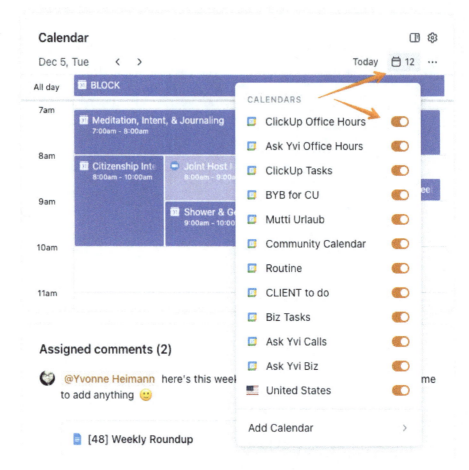

Figure 4.11 – Turn on Calendars

Click the calendar icon and select which Google Calendars to display.

If you have not connected your Google Calendar yet, you can do so by clicking on the Add Calendar menu item at the bottom and following the instructions.

Now that we have that taken care of, you can go ahead and change the due dates and times of the tasks you want to take care of today (or this week) in your My Work list to add them to today's calendar view to schedule and plan your workday (or workweek).

I also like to add my immediate tasks to the Task Tray in the bottom right. This allows me to easily access them throughout the day while I'm working on them, not needing to click back and forth within ClickUp or leaving multiple task tabs open.

You can easily add tasks to your Tray by opening the task and:

1. Click on the three dots to open the task menu.
2. Choose Add to.
3. Click Add to Tray.

As shown in *Figure 4.12*:

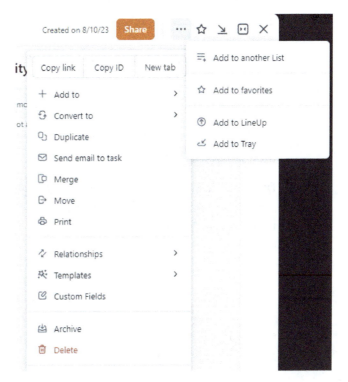

Figure 4.12 – Add a Task to Tray

This is how my clients and I start every productive day.

The ones extra productive don't even use the three dots, but rather the down arrow which does "minimize Task" into the task tray ;)

It most certainly is a new habit to develop, and it might take a few tries to make it a consistent habit. I promise it's worth the effort and will help you to stay on track with your priorities every day!

Summary

This concludes what you need to do to get yourself started in ClickUp all while avoiding productivity pitfalls. This chapter covered navigating ClickUp to personalizing your workspace and unlocking additional features followed by the most important best practices.

With this, you now have a strong foundation and are ready to dive deeper into ClickUp!

In the following chapters, we will take a closer look at how you can implement all this knowledge by use of case-specific examples.

You will learn how to use ClickUp's hierarchy based on your type of business model. We will take a closer look at custom fields and all the data they can manage for you.

Quickly followed by Custom Views and how to set them up. I know, you are waiting for this one after I teased you so much with Custom View magic in this chapter. You're so close, hang in there!

CHAPTER 5

Structuring Your ClickUp Workspace

You have already seen the many ways ClickUp can be customized to your specific needs and workflows – and structuring your ClickUp workspace is no exception! There are a lot of options to choose from.

One thing stays the same though! ***Your Workspace hierarchy should be client-focused, not process-focused.***

Now, what do I mean by that? It means we are building out ClickUp's Space and Folder structure, starting with the client as you'll see here shortly. We will not start with our deliverables (*when I say deliverables, it is the services that you provide*).

For example, deliverables could be:

- Social Media Management
- Virtual Assistant Services
- Web Design
- Podcast Production
- Video Editing
- Bookkeeping Services
- Coaching & Consulting
- A Course
- A Group Coaching Program
- And many more..

We do not want to think about all the nitty-gritty details of what needs to get done. We want to prioritize WHO we are doing it for. From there, we'll look at your offers and then build out the processes to get the deliverables done!

Let's dive into it, shall we?

Technical requirements

This far in the book, I do expect that you have read the previous chapters and be able to find your way around ClickUp. You should also have a clear understanding of the best practices that I covered in *Chapter 4*. If you know the difference between a Status and a Stage in ClickUp, you may proceed. You don't?? Please go back to *Chapter 4* and we'll regroup here once you're done.

Are we all set?

Great, let's talk about ClickUp's hierarchy and how to use it to structure your Workspace!

Structuring Your ClickUp Workspace

When it comes to structuring your ClickUp Workspace there are 3 major ways to do so.

Variation #1: Your client is handled on a Space level

Variation #2: Your client is handled on a Folder level

Variation #3: Your client is handled on a List level

Not sure what I'm talking about? You better go back to *Chapter 1* and revisit the ClickUp hierarchy ;)

If you know the ClickUp hierarchy enough to differentiate each level from the next, then here's how you can set up your ClickUp Workspace based on your business type.

Spaces every ClickUp Workspace should have

Oh, before we jump into how different business types might need different setups in ClickUp, let's go over the 5 ClickUp Spaces every business should have.

Every business should have the Spaces you can see in the image below.

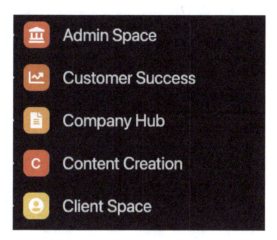

Figure 5.1 - Spaces every ClickUp Workspace should have

Admin Space

This is your ClickUp Space to house your operations. This is where you would folders and lists for things like:

- Your goals
- Miscellaneous admin tasks
- Your finances
- Recurring operational tasks

Customer Success

This is your Space for all the things that you do to ensure that all your clients are happy. No, not the services you deliver to your clients, but rather, the folders and lists to house all the other things that you do like:

- A CRM (Customer Relationship Management)
- A database of partners and associates supporting your business
- Customer support & client feedback
- How about a database of your favorite stores to get client gifts?

Company Hub

This houses all your company assets and supporting materials that your team needs to be the best that they can be.

- SOPs (Standard Operating Procedures) & Tool Wikis
- A database to record all the automations you might be running
- Various tools, softwares, or any trainings you own

Content Creation

This can also be called the Marketing Space. This is where you can manage your content creation and marketing efforts.

And last but not least your...

Client Space

This is where things start to change a little bit. Your Client Space in ClickUp is based on your business type. As mentioned at the beginning of this chapter, it can be set up in 3 different ways.

Let's start with our first setup!

Space = Client Structure

In this set up you organize your task and project management where every client gets their own Space within ClickUp.

It allows you to use the folder structure to organize different projects for each client, or for clients that have multiple entities.

For example, look at Disney - a major company that has multiple entities and projects going on all at the same time:

- Disney Movies & Shows
- Disney Parks
- Disney Marketing

I know, I went all fortune 500 on you with this example, but Disney is a great visual to explain to you when to use this setup.

If you are a video producer with Disney as your client, and you are capturing video footage to be used in some of their shows, to market their parks, as well as in their Social Media Marketing - this would probably be the time I would recommend this setup to you. The various folders separate all the different projects and help you not get mixed up. That's because every project gets its own folder, so it is neatly presented even with all the stuff going on at the same time.

Important Note

I rarely recommend this structure! This way of setting up ClickUp is best suited for companies with a small count of high-touch clients. This setup is quite involved and granular. It does work well for companies that run multiple projects per client: like an event company running multiple events every year for each client. This could also work well for an editor managing multiple book projects for the same client or an Airbnb manager servicing multiple properties for each property owner.

What it comes down to is that this setup is highly involved and only needed with Enterprise-size clients that you have enterprise-size involvement.

Often times though, even my Enterprise clients opted for the Folder = Client structure that we'll be talking about in the next section. However, I am committed to showing you all the options, and even though I don't recommend this setup to everyone, there are a few clients that have reaped its benefits. I want to make sure you know about it and can make an educated decision if this might be the right one for you.

You can see the general structure for this setup in the image below.

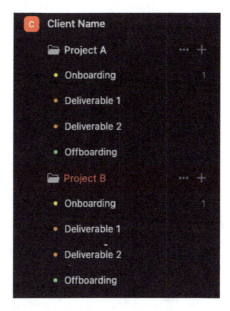

Figure 5.2 – Space = Client ClickUp Structure

The setup framework is as follows:

- Space = Client
  - Folder = Project
    - List = Services & Deliverable Types
      - Task = Deliverables
        - Subtasks & Checklists = Process

Folder = Client Structure

This is the most common way of setting up ClickUp and the framework I recommend to 95% of my clients and my YouTube audience.

In this setup, we go one layer down in ClickUp's hierarchy and each client gets their own folder in our client Space.

We have one Space in ClickUp that is our Deliverables or Client Space. This Client Space holds all the information of all our clients.

To be able to distinguish and separate each client from each other, we set up every client with their own folder in this Client Space.

The Lists needed for each client are determined by your deliverables as well as the client experience you want to deliver.

Looking at *Figure 5.3* below you can see some examples of Lists you might want to include in this kind of setup.

- **ClickUp Training:** if your client will be working with you in ClickUp, make sure they have the resources and knowledge to be able to confidently do so.

- **Client Training:** do you have communication guidelines, or maybe you help your clients run their business? This is the List where you would add tasks and links to show them how all that works.

- **Client Hub:** if you are tasking your clients directly in ClickUp, this is the list to do so in. It allows you to invite your client as a guest and ensure they won't see any of your internal tasks happening in any of the other lists.

- **Client Assets:** this is an important list for Social Media Managers, Web Designers, Videographers, and the likes. Use this list to collect and have easy access to all your client's HEX colors, brand details, and templates.

- **Services/Deliverables:** these are the lists where most of your doing your thing will happen. Add a list for every service you are delivering for your clients.

- **Onboarding/Offboarding:** these are the lists where your customer experience magic is found! Make sure to add tasks that ensure a smooth and enjoyable experience for your clients, which would make them want to continue working with you or work with you again in the future.

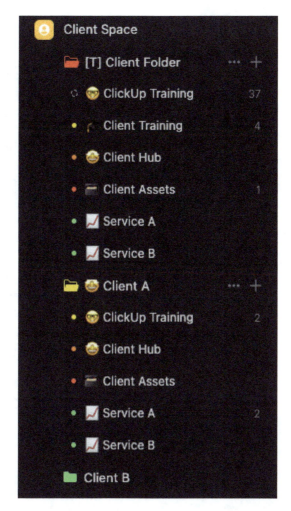

Figure 5.3 - Folder = Client ClickUp Structure

The setup framework is as followed:

- Space = All Client
  - Folder = Each Client
    - List = Services & Deliverable Types
      - Task = Deliverables
        - Subtasks & Checklists = Process

At the end of this chapter, you will find specific use case examples, so don't worry if this feels like a lot right now and you are wondering how to best implement these setups for your business. By the time you finish this chapter, you should have your options sorted out and choose which one fits your business or project needs best.

To recap, we've looked at the **Space = Client** and the **Folder = Client** setup. We just have one more variation for structuring your ClickUp before taking a closer look at specific use cases!

List = Client Structure

The setup is perfect for Entrepreneurs and businesses that has an ever-evolving collection of services for their clients.

One of these kinds of Entrepreneurs could be a virtual assistant that offers help with admin work. This type of work can be a variety of tasks and is often a collection of so many different smaller and more involved tasks that can change week by week.

As you can see in the image below, you can have a Client Work folder and each client has their own list in that folder.

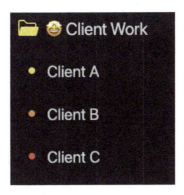

Figure 5.4 - List = Client ClickUp Structure

- Space = Work To Do
  - Folder = All Clients
    - List = Each Client
      - Task = Deliverables
        - Subtasks & Checklists = Process

Now that you understand the three approaches to structuring your ClickUp hierarchy, here are two specific use cases that you can emulate depending on your niche.

So, both of these follow my recommended way to structure your ClickUp Workspace: ***Folder = Client Structure***.

Use Case: Marketing Agency

Zenpilot is the leading implementor of ClickUp for agencies worldwide and you get to see a little of that magic. You are getting an exclusive behind-the-scenes look at how one of the biggest agency consultants handles their clients ClickUp built out.

Zenpilot follows the same kind of framework I mention in my ***Must Have 5 Spaces in ClickUp YouTube video*** that you will catch a glimpse of throughout this book (*and in all the use cases sometimes just named a bit differently*).

Based on *Figure 5.5*, you can see how Zenpilot has named and managed their 5 ClickUp Spaces for agencies.

Figure 5.5 - Agency Overview

In this use case for a ClickUp agency setup you see:

- **Growth:** houses the agencies marketing & sales tasks
- **Delivery:** aka the agencies' client work
- **Operations:** as in keeps the agency running
- **CRM:** manages the agency leads and deals
- **Process Library:** to manage the agencies templates and processes

Let's take a closer look at our first space: Growth, shall we?

Growth

As you can see in *Figure 5.6* below, the agency Growth space in ClickUp is separated into folders: one for marketing and one for sales.

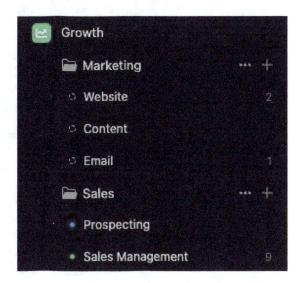

Figure 5.6 - Agency Growth

The marketing folder holds the agency's marketing tasks like web design content and email marketing. Whereas the sales folder holds your prospecting and Sales Management resources and tasks.

Delivery

Growing your agency is great, but you also have to deliver on your promise. This is where the delivery space comes into play as you can see in the image below.

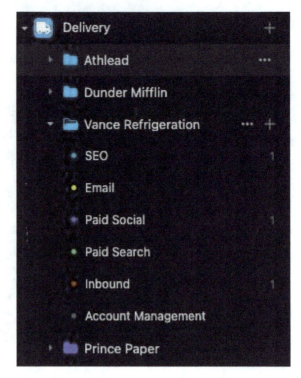

Figure 5.7 - Agency Delivery

As you can see the delivery space follows the Folder = Client structure we covered early in this chapter. It's really one of the easiest ways to manage your clients within ClickUp, and is also the most common way of setting up a ClickUp client space.

Within the clan folder you can see if move to the list based on the services the agency delivers. In this case:

- SEO
- Email
- PaidSsocial
- Paid Search
- Inbound

Plus, a list to handle general account management.

When wanting to start an agency there are a lot of operational tasks that are happening. As you can see in the *Figure 5.8* below there are way more operational tasks to be managed than there would be for a Solopreneur setup.

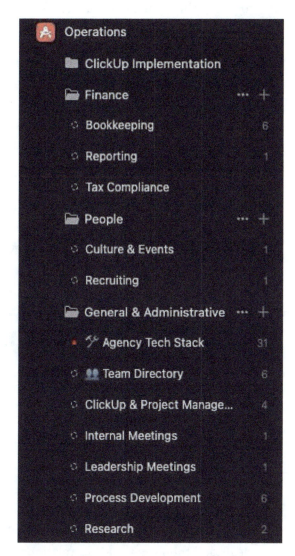

Figure 5.8 - Agency Operations

Here in Zenpilots framework you can see a full day of 4 ClickUp Implementation which houses tasks specific to implementing new ClickUp workflows and processes for the agency.

You will also find a Finance folder that houses lists for your general bookkeeping, reporting, as well as tax compliance tasks.

Another thing to bear in mind when running an agency is you don't want to forget about the human aspect. This is where the people folder comes in with lists to manage team events as well as recruiting.

Finally, to round up the agency operations space Zenpilot implements a general and administrative folder that houses the team directory, the agency's tech stack, meeting notes, as well as process development and research.

Now that I know that the team is taken care of, let's move on to make sure that the leads are also tended to. As you can see in the image below the CRM space does exactly that.

Figure 5.9 - Agency CRM

The agency CRM space has three lists:

- Deals
- Companies
- Contacts

Running your agency's CRM this way allows you to easily see all of your deals and then use ClickUp's relationship feature to connect the company and contact information to the deal. You will read more about the relationship custom field in *Chapter 6.*

As I mentioned before, there are a lot of processes involved when it comes to running an agency. Zenpilot's last agency space is called the Process Library and as you can see on *Figure 5.10*, it acts as their internal resource repository.

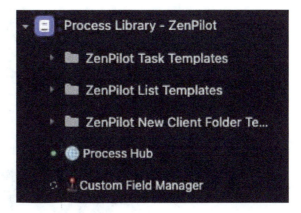

Figure 5.10 - Agency Process Library

This process Library houses multiple folders to manage all your different types of templates. It also houses your client folder template which allows you to easily duplicate your complete client setup.

In addition to that, they also have 2 lists: one is your Process Hub that houses your process maps, and the other is a list that helps manage their custom fields.

Not all of you want to run a full-fledged agency, and that's okay! Up next, we'll take a look at what ClickUp looks like all set up for a Business Coach.

Use Case: Business Coach

Yes, you are getting a special look underneath the hood of AskYvi.com and yours truly. This setup applies to any kind of professional service. In my specific case, as I work in my clients' space, I have changed my approach to have the client folder in my clients' ClickUp Workspace – but the choice is up to you. More on client management towards the end of this use case example!

Let's start with the big picture... What do we actually need?

As you can see in *Figure 5.11* below there's quite a few things going on.

Figure 5.11 - Biz Coach Overview

This workspace framework closely follows what I talked about in depth in my **Must Have 5 Spaces in ClickUp** YouTube video. You will see throughout this book and in all the use cases that all come back to these five ClickUp Spaces, sometimes named differently.

Let's take a look at how I customized and added to those 5 basic spaces to run my own business:

- **Ask Yvi Admin:** our admin tasks.
- **Customer Success:** making clients happy, this is not your deliverables but rather testimonials and support.
- **Content Creation:** ideation and creation of all the things I share on social media.
- **Ask Yvi Hub:** our SOPs and Wikis.
- **Boss Your Business Library:** where we manage course content and resources.
- **Ask Yvi Clients:** my client space, I now import this into my clients ClickUp Workspace.
- **Community Management:** managing and supporting my community.

Ask Yvi Admin

As a coach, consultant, or professional service provider, in general, there is a lot going on in your business. Keeping your admin tasks as well as your goals and objectives nice and tidy allows you to focus on what's most important - helping your clients be awesome! After all, no one wants to spend all their days doing admin work, right?

As you can see in *Figure 5.12* below, we here at Ask Yvi have a few folders in our admin space.

Figure 5.12 - Biz Coach Admin Space

Our admin space is separated into three folders:

- **Biz:** where we house ur actual admin tasks
- **Goals:** what is our mission and vision, the values we stand for, and the objective & Key Results (OKR) we want to achieve
- **Biz Finances:** is a space that reminds me when payments are due ;)

Let's take a little closer look at the Biz folder!

Here you see the Misc Admin list, which is my list for all these random "*I don't know where to put this*" tasks.

Right after that, you see the Biz Routine list. You can use this list for, as the name says, business routines. No matter if it is daily, weekly, monthly, quarterly, or annual tasks - this is their home. This list would house tasks like bookkeeping, and website maintenance reminders. If you follow Profit First for your finances your profit allocation task would go here too.

The Improvements list is where all the ideas to improve your business should go. A little pro tip: you can add a recurring quarterly task in your Biz Routine list to evaluate and plan the implementation of your latest improvements ;)

Last but not least, the Personal list is where you would add your non-business to-do list, maybe you want to keep track of your upcoming appointments or even plan your next grocery run.

Customer Success

Now that we have our admin tasks squared away, let's look at the Customer Success Space you can see in the image below.

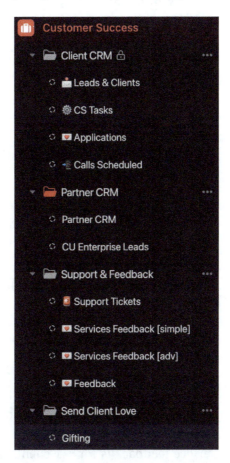

Figure 5.13 - Biz Coach Customer Success Space

The first folder you'll see is my CRM. You will need to decide for yourself if a ClickUp CRM is applicable to what you are trying to build. Managing leads and clients is simple here at Ask Yvi and I don't particularly work with a massive number of 1:1 clients, so if you have a lot of clients or even a sales team, this setup might not be for you.

I dive really deep into this **CRM setup in this video** which will help you figure out if implementing a ClickUp CRM for your business would be a good idea.

The thing is, I often work with a lot of people online. You might have heard about the ClickUp Vetted Consultant Program; that's where I collaborate with quite a few of my fellow consultants when we reach maximum capacity, or if a client needs something very niche specific that's not in my current service offerings.

Because this requires the time, effort, and potentially resources of several professionals, it's important that I have a Partner CRM to refer to with all my partners' information, who they serve, and what they offer.

As ClickUp's Evangelist, I often get a lot of questions and leads when it comes to ClickUp's Enterprise plan. We decided internally to simplify things and add a list to manage those leads so my trusted sales agent, Bill, has all the information he needs to serve my community the best way possible during this process.

When you are evaluating whether or not you need or even want these two folders in your workspace, think about how many clients you manage and/or who you potentially would be collaborating with to give your leads the best solution possible.

Up next is the Support & Feedback folder which is a collection of lists for different offers.

My Support Tickets List collects information from our support form and acts as a ticketing system for our digital client support tickets.

Service feedback is for 1:1 clients, and those have been separated into a quick check-in (simple) feedback form as well as an advance "end of job" feedback form. Yes, all these are managed through a form here my clients submit their feedback in ;) So, I don't have to manually do anything.

Quick side story, the last 2 lists in *Figure 5.13*? That was crazy. You have no idea how long it took me to realize that I needed an efficient way to collect feedback and testimonials! (*Did I just hear you laugh a bit? It's okay, I deserved that!*)

Yes, I know how ridiculous it is that the Queen of Business Efficiency completely missed that one! So, hey, please do me a favor! Implement this right now, especially if you don't have a straightforward way to collect testimonials or get feedback when you're offboarding clients.

The Feedback list follows the same setup but is for courses and templates.

The last folder is what I call Send Client Love, it's the Ask Yvi gifting list. Here we collect gifting ideas and links for when we want to send out goodies to our clients.

Content Creation

Clients don't just magically show up. I actually have to be out there and show up first. I do that by intentionally and consistently creating content that my audience can learn from, feel inspired by, or get a good laugh or two. We expand the Ask yvi multiverse by repurposing content, optimizing each of them for several different platforms.

If you refer to the figure below, you'll see that under the Content Creation Space, I have a Creation Folder – Boss Your Business Podcast Folder – and ClickUp Book Folder.

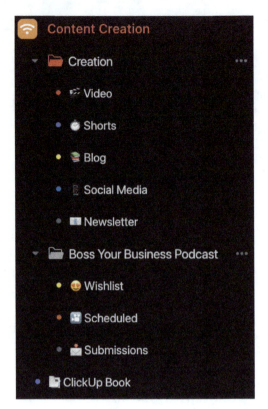

Figure 5.14 - Biz Coach Content Creation Space

The Creation folder is separated in our case into 5 key focuses: Video, shorts, blog, social media, and newsletter.

Next, we have the Boss Your Business Podcast folder, which houses our podcast essentials such as who we want to guest on the show, who has already scheduled an episode with us, and pending guest applications.

- **Wishlist:** housing guests I would like on my podcast
- **Scheduled:** episode & guest that have been scheduled to record
- **Submissions:** applications of guests that would like to be on our show

You can learn more about how we keep managing and repurposing a podcast really simple right here in this YouTube Playlist.

Lastly, the ClickUp book folder, which by some miracle you are reading right now!

<table>
<tr><td>Note</td></tr>
<tr><td>For the most part, I think the creation folder is pretty self-explanatory, but if you would like to dive deeper into the processes that are happening in those lists, I got a YouTube playlist for you right here that covers everything about how we manage our content creation day to day.</td></tr>
</table>

Ask Yvi Hub

The next space in our Ask Yvi ClickUp Workspace is our company Hub which you can see in *Figure 5.15* below.

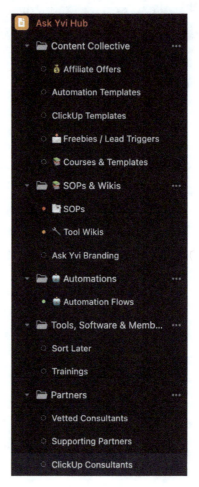

Figure 5.15 - Biz Coach Hub Space

As you can see, we've got a lot going on in the Ask Yvi hub. We are always evolving and adjusting our setup. I want to take this as a chance to remind you ClickUp is so versatile, it allows you to constantly adjust and update your setup if needed.

And while this space is probably the messiest in our workspace right now, it's important to remember that even the most advanced users & consultants out there do not have an ultra-perfect setup!

Say it with me, "Done and usable is always better than perfect."

Here's a more comprehensive look at what's going on in the Ask Yvi Hub:

- The **Content Collective folder** is our space to collect all kinds of different links. No matter if it's our affiliate links, make.com automation templates to be shared with clients or in courses, easy links to the ClickUp templates we offer, or any kind of freebies or courses.

  Think of this as your database of links. Your folder to collect everything you sell and share so your VA knows exactly what to promote in that social media post of yours and which link is the right one to use.

- The **SOP and Wiki folder** houses your standard operations and you tool Wikis. In addition to that, we also added a list that houses Ask Yvi's branding assets - from social media post templates to hex codes everything is right in there.

- **Automations folder** documents how our automations are currently set up.

- How often has your Virtual Assistant or team asked you which tools you have available in your company? Or maybe they wanted to advance themselves and get upskill training?

  The **Tools, Software, and Membership folder** is for exactly that! It's where we store training and other resources that we invested in and are available to your team. Plus, tools and software details that we've bought licenses for.

- The last folder is in the Ask Yvi Hub space is our **Partner folder**. This is where we collect the information of our partners and collaborators. Most consultants I know don't just create content for social media, sometimes we collaborate and do special group coaching programs or courses. Having a Partner folder helps me keep track of everyone I have ever created resources with.

Content Creation

The Boss Your Business Library space houses my exclusive course and group coaching assets. As you can see in the image below there are quite a few elements that need to go into a setup like this.

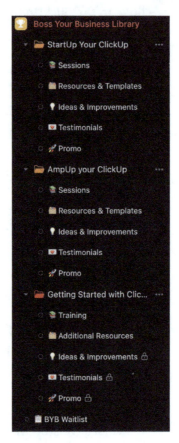

Figure 5.16 - Biz Coach Library Space

We have sorted the Boss Your Business Library space into multiple folders based on our two membership offers:

- StartUp Your ClickUp
- AmpUp Your ClickUp

Within those folders you will find lists that allow us to manage sessions, easily link resources and templates used in that membership, as well as a list that lets us collect ideas and improvements for that specific membership.

We also have a list to collect testimonials specifically to this offer as well as the promo assets.

Outside of the already existing offers, this space also houses a list that collects everybody that signed up for our Boss Your Business group coaching program waitlist.

Ask Yvi Clients

As you may or may not know, I still do work one-on-one with clients. This last space for our coaches and Consultants handles our client delivery. In my case, because I work to help my clients streamline their processes and workflows within ClickUp, I decided to move this space out of my own ClickUp workspace and into my clients' ClickUp workspace. If you are not a ClickUp consultant this framework and setup is the same for you - you would just simply keep it in your own workspace.

As you can see in image 5.17 below Ask Yvi Client Space is really simple and straightforward.

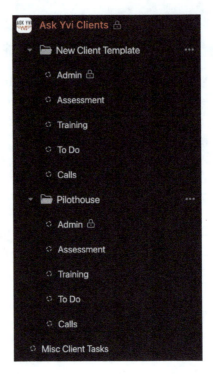

Figure 5.17 - Biz Coach Client Space

As mentioned so often in this chapter already, this is a Folder = Client framework.

- The **Admin list**, set to private so only I can see it, is for me and my team to handle admin tasks related to this client.
- Within the **Assessment list**, we are managing the team research and assessment of how they are doing within ClickUp right now. This allows me to determine where there might be knowledge gaps within the team, making it difficult for them to follow the processes.
- The **Training list** houses the basic ClickUp training to ensure every team member has a basic knowledge of how to maneuver with a ClickUp.
- The **To-Do list** houses the task management for me as well as the client to continuously move to the project further and not forget about any tasks we committed to.

- And as the name says the **Calls list** houses the recordings and transcriptions of all our calls.

If you are housing your client folders within your own workspace, there are often some tasks that are just popping up and don't really fit into this framework. To accommodate those random miscellaneous tasks, we added a **Misc Client Task list** right in our client space - easy to find and easy to manage.

AHHH... You made it, you made it! You made it through this big chapter on how to structure your ClickUp workspace. Go grab yourself a treat or coffee to celebrate, coz really, you deserve it! And while you're at it take a little bit of a brain break as I need to be back at 100% brain power for the next chapter when we are diving into ClickUp custom fields.

Community Management

Setting up a dedicated Community Management space in ClickUp can be a valuable way to streamline and organize various tasks related to managing and supporting your community. We primarily use this space to plan out community-specific content, events, and strategies that elevate the Ask Yvi community.

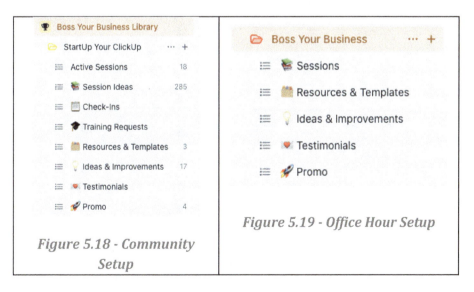

Figure 5.18 - Community Setup

Figure 5.19 - Office Hour Setup

Summary

In this chapter we took a closer look at the ClickUp hierarchy and how to use it to structure your own ClickUp workspace.

If you only take one thing from this chapter it should be that using the Folder = Client framework is the most common, most versatile, and easiest framework on how to set up your ClickUp.

Now that you have an understanding of the ClickUp hierarchy and the best way of structuring it, it is time for us to take a closer look at ClickUp custom fields and how to use them to add more functionality to your ClickUp spaces.

CHAPTER 6

ClickUp Custom Fields 101

You've already heard about ClickUp custom fields in the past chapters. It is finally time for us to explore the magic of ClickUp custom fields.

To put it simply, Custom Fields is where a lot of ClickUp's power and customization lies.

ClickUp custom fields allow you to collect, manage, and organize a lot of different types of data.

In past chapters, you have already received a nice taste of what is possible with ClickUp custom fields. So, in this chapter, we will be diving deeper into what custom fields are available to you, how to set them up, and use custom fields within your ClickUp workspace.

With these custom fields, you will not be limited to just managing tasks and projects, but also develop a powerful system for collecting data.

What You'll Learn:

- We'll first look at how to setup and add custom fields within ClickUp.
- And then we'll dive into the different types of custom fields that ClickUp offers. These range from text, dropdowns, numbers, checkboxes, people pickers, dates and much more!

By the end of this chapter, you will have a firm understanding of how ClickUp custom fields work and how they can help you unleash your workspace potential!

Technical requirements

Custom field usage is limited to 100 uses on the FREE ClickUp plan. Some of the more advanced custom Fields like custom task IDs are not available on the Unlimited or lower ClickUp plans.

Like I said previously, the moment you realize that you are seriously going to use ClickUp in your business, I always recommend upgrading to at least the Business plan to ensure you have all the features available to you without any limitations.

The book bonuses you can find at: https://askyvi.tips/SPMCBonus include a Price Estimator and maybe even some hidden deals for you ;)

Setting Up & Using ClickUp Custom Fields

The ClickUp custom fields feature is a ClickApp and as mentioned in *Chapter 3*, you need to turn it on in your ClickApps settings as shown in the image below.

Custom Fields

Add Custom Fields to your tasks to literally use ClickUp for anything: dates, phone numbers, emails, drop-downs, checkboxes, links, currencies, and numbers.
Learn more

Sort Custom Fields manually instead of alphabetically.

33 Spaces ⌄

Figure 6.1 - ClickUp Custom Field ClickApp

Once you get the ClickUp custom fields feature turned on in your ClickApps, many of the actual ClickUp custom field types need to be turned on through the ClickApps too, as shown in the image below using the example of ClickUp Custom Task IDs.

Custom Task IDs

Customize your task IDs to more easily reference them in ClickUp, in conversation, or via integrations.

Enable ClickApp

Figure 6.2 - Enable ClickUp Custom Field Type

If you are unfamiliar with the ClickApps in ClickUp, I recommend going back to *Chapter 3* and revisiting them. Once you have an understanding of ClickApps I recommend browsing through your ClickApp settings to get an idea of what ClickUp custom fields are mentioned within the ClickApps.

The Basics of Custom Fields

Custom fields help you organize projects, tasks, and subtasks with more precision. Additional data in ClickUp Custom fields makes it easier for everyone on your team to quickly understand what's going on in the project.

With ClickUp's advanced custom field options, you can attach additional information like project links, images, dates, and even text notes to any task. You can also set up formulas that calculate different values based on your data inputs.

Custom fields are incredibly versatile and allows you to use ClickUp more efficiently.

ClickUp custom fields closely follow the ClickUp hierarchy. Meaning a ClickUp custom field that is set up on the space level is available to all of the areas below - it will be available in all of the folders of that space as well as all of the lists within those folders and all of the tasks within those lists.

Important Note:

To keep your ClickUp custom fields nice and tidy, I always recommend starting to add your ClickUp custom fields on the lowest level in the ClickUp hierarchy possible.

Once a ClickUp custom field is set up you can add the same custom field to other areas through the custom field library - more on this later in this chapter.

To add a custom field in the list view, click the + icon on the top right of your ClickUp lists. This will open up the custom field menu as you can see in the image below.

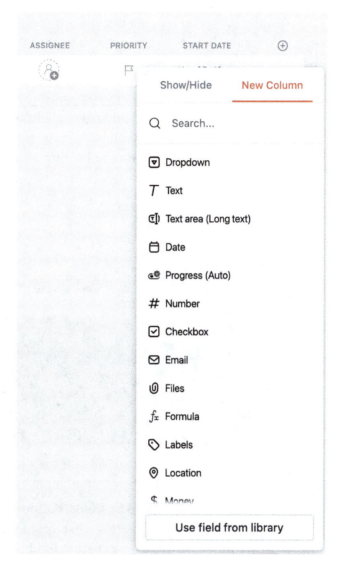

Figure 6.3 - Adding ClickUp Custom Fields

The **Show/Hide** part of menu will house a list of fields that are either standard to your ClickUp workspace as a whole or your custom fields already existing in this list location.

Under **New Column** you will find the types of custom fields activated in ClickApps and available to you.

Last but not least, if you have already set up a specific custom field in another location of your ClickUp workspace, e.g. another folder or list, you can find these by clicking the **"Use field from field library"** button at the bottom of this menu. This will allow you to add any existing custom field to this specific location.

Once you have one custom field in your task, you then can also add or edit your custom field right within the task itself. Simply open the task and find the custom field section right below the task description as shown in the image below.

Figure 6.4 - Adding ClickUp Custom Fields in a Task

Clicking the **+Add or edit fields** button with open the custom field list showing you all custom fields that exist for this task in its location. It will also allow you To add **new custom field**s by clicking the New custom field button. And as mentioned before you can **use an existing field** by adding it from the custom field library.

Now that we have the basics of custom fields down let's take a look at how to specifically use custom fields in ClickUp and what type of custom fields are actually available to you.

Using Custom Fields

The use cases of ClickUp custom Fields are broad and vary based on the type of custom fields you're using. One of the most commonly used ClickUp custom fields is the drop-down filled, which is also the one we are using for stages. If you don't know what I mean by stages, please revisit *Chapter 4 - ClickUp Best Practices* to get familiar with status vs stages in ClickUp.

Back to the ClickUp drop-down, it's a single select custom field, but there are also other custom fields that allow you to select multiple items from a list. Some custom fields are also able to manage multiple different types of numbers as well as different types of text fields.

We will also be looking at the more advanced ClickUp custom fields that allow you to build relationships between different tasks within your ClickUp, add formulas, calculate number fields, and much more.

Overall ClickUp custom fields are where you collect, manage, and connect data within your tasks. In the image below, you can see all of the custom field types available in ClickUp.

Figure 6.5 - All ClickUp Custom Fields

As shown in *Figure 6.5*, you have quite a wide selection when it comes to custom fields options. Let's start with the standard fields available to you in ClickUp.

Standard Fields in ClickUp

Now, before we explore those custom fields that require specific set up and naming conventions, here are the standard custom fields that are available and can easily be added to any task (*in alphabetical order*):

- **Assign comments**: show you a count of open assigned comments in this task.
- **Assignee:** shows the avatar of the assignee of the task or subtask.

- **Comments:** shows the comment count for this task.
- **Created by:** shows the avatar of the person that created the task.
- **Custom task ID:** if turned on in ClickApps will show your custom task ID.
- **Date closed:** the date when this task was closed/completed.
- **Date created:** the date when this task was created.
- **Date updated:** the date when this task was last updated.
- **Dependencies:** shows what other task/s are being blocked by this task or are blocking this task.
- **Due date:** the date when this is task due by.
- **Latest comment:** what was the latest comment on this task.
- **Linked docs:** what documents are linked to this task.
- **Lists:** indicates the lists this task is in.
- **Priority:** give your tasks a priority flag indicating: Low, Normal, High, or Urgent.
- **Pull Requests:** is connected to the ClickUp Bitbucket integration for Pull Requests.
- **Sprints:** lets you add this task to a sprint.
- **Sprint Points:** shows the amount of sprint points for this task.
- **Start date:** when is the task start date.
- **Status:** what's the status of this task.
- **Task ID:** shows the standard ClickUp task ID.
- **Time tracked:** shows the time tracked for this task.
- **Total time in Status:** how long has this task been in this status.

These are all standard fields available to you within your ClickUp workspace. You can Show/Hide them in the list menu as explained earlier in this chapter.

Remember: Some of these might need to be turned on in your ClickApp settings first.

Now that you know what standard fields are available to you, let's take a look at some of the simple custom fields in ClickUp!

Beginner Custom Fields

These are the most commonly used custom fields in ClickUp, easy to use and straight away let you sort and add additional information to your task. Let's start with our first custom field types available to you in ClickUp. In the image below you'll see the first nine types we'll be talking about.

Figure 6.6 - Beginner ClickUp Custom Fields

Checkbox

As the name already implies, this is a simple yes-no type custom field. To be completely honest, we here at AskYvi.com do not use this specific custom field, ever. We would rather use the checklist option within the task itself for our workflows. However, it can be a helpful custom field to easily be able to display if something is approved and checked off.

Date

This is a custom field similar to your due date field in ClickUp. It is, however, not connected to your notifications and will not automatically notify you if this date is reached.

We often use this custom field in content creation to be able to easily showcase different dates in the content creation process.

For example, using the date custom field to display the date of blog post published, YouTube video published, and the social media evergreen start date. If you are trying to wrap your head around this content repurposing process and the use of the custom date fields

I have a video where *I talk about this process right here for you.*

Dropdown

Custom fields are probably our most used type of custom field within ClickUp. Drop down custom Fields a single select option and we use it to indicate stages our tasks go through (*see chapter 4 - Best Practices*). This custom field can also be used for many other use case scenarios that need a single select option.

Best use case would be:

- Daily, weekly, monthly, quarterly, and annual: Allowing you to sort your recurring tasks by their recurrency.

- ClickUp VC Program, Website, Referral, YouTube: Letting you indicate where a lead came from in your ClickUp CRM set up.

- Draft, Proof, Approved, Ready: To indicate the progression of your asset development.

Email

This is a custom field that ensures that the entry is an email address and easily lets you click on the said email address to email them. You do have to have a default email app set up on your computer for this to work properly.

It's also the one used in the ClickUp email feature that allows you to email people right from your task comment section or in the native ClickUp email automation.

Files

This allows you to upload files to your ClickUp task. These files will show up at the bottom of the task as attachments.

To upload files, simply click the files icon or the plus icon if you already have attached files. This custom field will allow you to upload files from your local hard drive or your cloud storage services.

Label

are similar to tags and allow you to choose multiple items from the tags list. You can group and sword your views by labels. We often use this custom field to indicate:

- *Size of video: 1920x1080, 1080x1080, 1080x19020*
- *Size of graphics needed: feed, story, thumbnail*

Or any similar use cases where you need a multitude of versions or answers.

Location

Think of this custom field as Google Maps straight up in your ClickUp. This custom field will format addresses based on Google Maps and is the custom field that ClickUp's map view relies on for its magic.

Money

This automatically formats the number entered in this custom field into any currency. When adding or editing this custom field, you will see a currency drop-down field in its settings for you to choose which currency you would like to show.

When you look back up on *Figure 6.6*, you will also see that you can also calculate the sum, average, or range of money custom field columns, which will show up at the bottom of the column.

Number

This custom field is a general numbers field for numbers that do not have a specific indicator. And as you can see in *Figure 6.6* above the number custom field column can be calculated as sum, average, or range just like the money custom field.

Now that we have the first batch of ClickUp custom fields done, let me introduce you to the next 8 types of custom fields shown in the image below.

Figure 6.7 - Beginner ClickUp Custom Fields

People

This custom field allows you to pick people and teams. When setting up this ClickUp custom field, you will also have the choice of showing people from the entire workspace, show guests, or to include your ClickUp workspace teams.

We often use the people custom field within ClickUp when doing company evaluations to indicate who provided this feedback for the specific evaluation. This custom field is also helpful for work orders to indicate which team the work order is actually assigned to.

Phone

This is pretty straightforward and simple. This custom field formats the number entered into a phone number with country and area code. This will even show you a little flag based on the country code and clicking on that flag will let you change the country code for each phone number.

The most common use case scenario for this ClickUp custom field is probably a CRM set up right in ClickUp or a client database that houses your clients' phone numbers.

Progress (Auto)

This shows the progression of your task automatically. This progress tracks the completion of stop tasks, archived subtasks, checklist, and assigned comments. You get to choose which of these will automatically be tracked within the setup process of this custom field.

Within the setup process, you can also choose how to display tasks without any action items. You can choose if this non-action item task will display as 100% when the task is in a done status, display 100% complete in general, and displays as 0% completed. The most common setting would be to display it at 100% when the task is in a done status.

Rating

Custom fields in ClickUp come in really handy when using it for client feedback, company evaluation, and planning your own business improvements.

The Rating custom field in ClickUp allows you to choose from a wide variation of emojis. You can also set the emoji amount to anywhere between 1-5.

Let me show you my favorite use case in the image below.

Figure 6.8 - Using Ratings for your Business Improvement List

We love using the ratings ClickUp custom field within our Improvement list for Ask Yvi.

One set of emojis indicates the impact of this Improvement on my business. While the other set of emojis showcases the ease of implementation of this improvement. This way, we can visually tell if it's worth implementing this improvement or if it simply has no impact on our business or is just way too difficult to be worth the effort.

Text and Text Area

Text is a one-liner, short-form text field - think headline, while text area is a long-form text custom field within ClickUp - think story.

The different use cases between the two text fields are with the one-liner ClickUp text field. We often use that as a quick short answer. Whereas the text area is more of a long-form written content field.

Website

Even though it is called Website, it is actually a URL field. You can use this ClickUp custom field for any type of URL. We use this field to link any kind of external assets such as SOPs housed on other platforms or Google Drive folders for digital assets.

You can also easily store internal website links, like documents in ClickUp.

By using the Website Custom Field, team members can quickly see where related resources are stored. This eliminates the need for back-and-forth searching or endless scrolling through long lists.

All of these custom fields within ClickUp are pretty easy to understand. Now, let's take a look at some of the advanced custom fields that can supercharge your ClickUp.

Advanced Custom Fields

ClickUp Advanced Custom fields like relationships and rollup fields, lets you get even more granular control over your content. You can use them to relate projects, tasks, and documents together or to see the most important data in one place with rollup fields.

This helps keep the data consistent across multiple projects at once and also makes it easier for teams to quickly access key information from any project they may need.

Additionally, these fields can be used for reporting purposes as well as being able to group related items together for better organization.

Relationships

The easiest use-case to explain the relationship custom field in ClickUp is a CRM setup, which you can learn more about and see an example of in this video of mine: https://youtu.be/BTeiFTlBiOg.

You can use the relationship custom field to manage any type of relationship between two objects/ClickUp tasks (*e.g., clients and projects, customers and leads, support tickets, and user*).

You can create two types of Custom Relationships:

- Link any task in your Workspace regardless of location.
- Link tasks from a specific List, which means you set a relationship between two lists and then link tasks from either List to each other.

When you link tasks from a specific list you can even show their Custom Fields on the other related task!

To really give you a good understanding of the power of the relationship custom field, let's look at the image below.

Figure 6.9 - ClickUp Custom Relationship Field Example

This is a database-type CRM set up in ClickUp. As you can see, we have three different lists for different types of clients: Leads, Active Clients, and Past clients.

This folder also has three lists to house supporting information:

- **Services**, as in your service offerings
- **Contacts**, as in all the people in the companies you are in contact with
- **Companies**, and the companies you work with

What the relationship custom field allows us to do is to link tasks from one list to another, therefore easily connecting the information of these tasks.

Let's make understanding all these easier in the example above in *Figure 6.9.*

As you can see, we are on the Contacts list, which houses all of the people/contacts we might be in contact with at any given time.

Now, we might be in contact with multiple people that are working in the same company. To be able to connect all those people to the company that they belong to and be able to link all of the company information, we add a relationship field that is connected to the company list.

This allows us to pull in the tasks from the Companies list - see how it says Ask Yvi in the pop-up?

Now that the data in these two lists is connected through the relationship field, you can easily see all the company information. Simply click on the company once it is added in the relationship field.

As shown in Figure 6.9, clicking Ask Yvi in the relationship field will open up a pop-up window that shows a list of all of the companies within the company relationship field.

By clicking on one of those company relationship custom fields, which in this case is Ask Yvi, it will open up the Ask Yvi task within the company list and show you all of the information associated with this task.

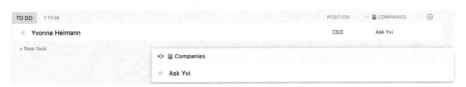

Figure 6.10 - ClickUp Custom Relationship Field Use

This now allows you to see information in a multitude of locations without having to click throughout your whole workspace.

Let's finish thinking through this use case:

- You have your CRM right here in ClickUp.
- You have your contacts and Company list.
- You can now easily add company information to multiple people without having to add the specific company information manually to each one of those people over and over again.

Can you imagine all these custom fields and all the copy and paste happening just to have the shipping address and billing email noted in all those contacts?

This relationship field within ClickUp also allows you to update the company information and show the updated information for all of the people connected to this company without ever having to update anything within those contacts.

You just update the information in the company-specific task and due to the information being linked in the relationship field, everything automatically shows the current information.

Now that we have the contact information management down right here in our ClickUp CRM, next on our list is to take a look at how to manage client value.

Rollup

This is where the Rollup custom field comes into play.

Take another quick little look at Figure 6.9 above.

In this example of a CRM setup, we not only have company and contact information.

This setup also has a list of your services. In this Services list, you would house your different services and each task is one service. The cost of the service would be housed in a money custom field.

For us to easily see the value of each client we need to follow the same setup as we did before for our contacts. Add your custom relationship field to your active Client List and set up the custom relationship field connecting it to your services list as you can see in the image below.

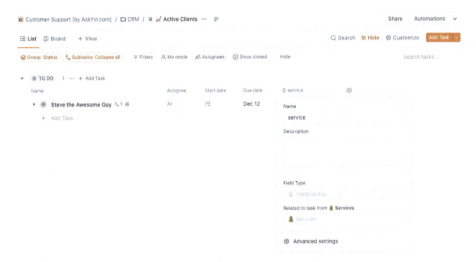

Figure 6.11 - ClickUp Rollup Custom Field

As you can see custom rollup fields are closely related to your relationship field. In our use-case example, we chose the sum off the money field we used in our services list. This now allows us to easily see the total value of each client as shown in the image below.

6.12 - ClickUp Rollup Custom Field / Service List

This is just a quick look into which services this client hired us for and what the total value of this client is.

You've seen how easy it is to get some basic calculations in number field columns or roll-up fields done. What about some advanced calculations in rows though?

Formula

This is where the formula custom field is used.

Let's start with some formula field basics:

Formula fields can be added anywhere in your ClickUp hierarchy. However, your formula fields cannot be moved to any other location.

Formula fields and the edits you make in a formula field apply to the entire column of tasks in the location you add the formula field.

Within the formula field you can make calculations using the following ClickUp fields:

- Number Custom Fields
- Currency Custom Fields
- Dropdown Custom Fields that only use numbers
- Date Custom Fields
- Start Date & Due Date
- Date Created
- Date Started
- Date Updated
- Date Closed
- Time Tracked (in hours)
- Time Estimated (in hours)

Using any of these fields above you now can easily build simple formula fields like the one in the image below.

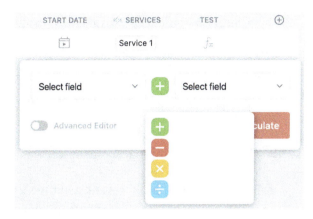

6.13 - ClickUp Simple Formula

The magic doesn't stop here though!

Turning on the advanced editor by simply flipping the switch in your formula field settings you will suddenly see the advanced formula functions displayed in the image below.

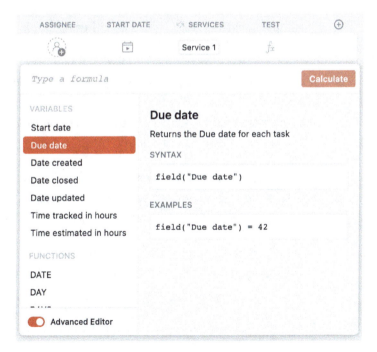

6.14 - ClickUp Advanced Formula

So many possibilities!! Calculating how many hours you have left on a project, profit, and so much more.

You can find a list with all the advanced functions and syntax information right here: https://help.clickup.com/hc/en-us/articles/6308656424983-Formula-Fields

This was an action-packed chapter, wasn't it?

Let's recaffeinate and revisit what we learned before diving into the next chapter and learning about custom views in ClickUp.

Summary

As you've seen in this chapter, ClickUp Custom Fields are versatile and powerful. Take a moment to revisit this chapter and open up your ClickUp to put what you've learned into practice.

If you'd like to get the CRM template shown in this chapter, you can grab that with all your other book bonuses right here: https://askyvi.tips/SPMCBonus.

Having a great understanding of the different types and use-cases of ClickUp Custom Fields will make understanding and following along with the rest of this book so much easier as many ClickUp implementations heavily rely on custom fields.

We will also mention custom fields in Chapter 7 as Custom Views allow us to build task views for specific use cases. Some of which might be sorted or grouped by one or more of the custom field types you just learned about.

Stay tuned as we dive even further into customizing ClickUp to your specific needs!

ClickUp Custom Views 101

I've mentioned this before, and you've also seen a sneak peek of ClickUp's powerful custom views in the previous chapters. Now it's time to focus on how to efficiently use and maximize this functionality to customize your workspace.

Custom views are truly one of the most useful features in ClickUp for tailoring what you see to match your needs and specific use cases. In this chapter, we'll explore even more fun possibilities with custom views!

Starting with the basics of setting up views from scratch or editing existing views, then we'll look at unique view types like form and embedded views.

One of the best parts of custom views is the ability to template, save, and lock views to make your personal workflow as well as your team's day to day a breeze.

By the end of this chapter, you'll have the knowledge to create custom views that streamline your productivity. You'll be able to craft the perfect set up for every situation.

Get ready to supercharge your workspace with some custom views magic!

Technical requirements

Custom view usage has some limitations based on your plan and the type of view you are using. For example, Map view is not available on the FREE plan, and Whiteboard view is limited on the Unlimited plan and below.

Please refer to the ClickUp pricing page for more details.

As I stated in previous chapters, the moment you begin seriously considering ClickUp for your business, I always recommend upgrading to at least the Business plan to ensure you have all the features available to you without any limitations.

The book bonuses you can find at: https://askyvi.tips/SPMCBonus include a Price Estimator and maybe even some hidden deals for you ;)

The Basic of Custom Views

You have already learned about the different types of custom views in *Chapter 1*. If you don't remember, now is a good time to get a refresher on that chapter before we learn more about how to create and customize views from scratch to match your unique workflow needs.

The key to efficiently using custom views is understanding that they allow you to shape exactly what information you see in ClickUp. You can customize columns, filters, sorting, grouping - pretty much anything and everything to really build views for all your use cases.

Let's start with the basics of building a view.

You can create a view at the workspace, folder, list, or board level. As always, views follow the ClickUp hierarchy - that means if you'd like to show tasks and assets that are housed in multiple locations, you will need to go up the hierarchy to the level that has access to all those locations.

Maybe you set up that custom view on list level - as all tasks you want to show are in that list.

Or it could be a folder - if it holds all the lists you need access to.

It also could be housed in a space - if it holds all the folders and lists that you'd like to include.

Or maybe it needs to be a custom view in your Everything level to include your whole Workspace.

> **Important Note:**
>
> If your custom views include custom fields REMEMBER that custom fields also follow the ClickUp hierarchy! So, if you set up a custom view on the Everything level and you bring custom fields up from a lower level to show in your Everything custom view... Those custom fields now will be on EVERY task throughout your whole workspace!

You've already learned about the different types of custom views and how to add them in *Chapter 1*. Let's get a closer look into what's possible to make your everyday task views like list and board view super insightful.

Many of these settings are also available in calendar, workload, table, and the other tasks views. I'll be using the ClickUp list view in this chapter to showcase all these settings.

As you can see in *Figure 7.1*, when you look at the top of your List there are a few buttons that allow you to group and filter your tasks as well as change a few other settings to determine what will be shown in the List.

Everything

7.1 - ClickUp Custom View Settings

Let's start with Grouping.

Grouping Tasks allows you to organize your tasks in different ways to get a helpful perspective. Some common options are by:

- **Assignee** - help identify workload.
- **Status** - like To Do, In Progress, etc. to give you a process status overview.
- **Due Date** - easily see what's due when, and has to be taken care of first.
- **Custom Field** - to see task stages, specific types of deliverables, and others.

Now if you look at *Figure 7.2*, in addition to these you can also group by List. This will make your chosen grouping stay within a nice little box - visually showing you the list where your tasks are housed first.

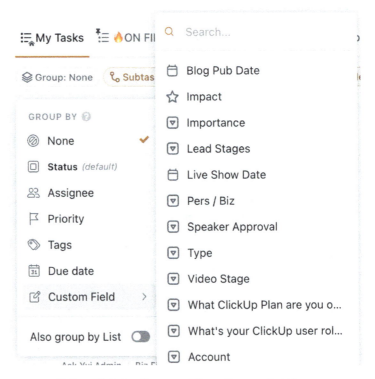

7.2 - ClickUp Custom View Group Settings

The second button gives you control over how subtasks are displayed.

There are three view options:

- **Collapse all** - Subtasks are hidden under their parent task. Simply click the little arrow on the left side of the task name to open up the subtask. This setting is great for a high-level compact view.

- **Expanded all** - All subtasks are shown indented under their parent task. This allows you to see the full task hierarchy at a glance.

- **As separate tasks** - Subtasks display as individual tasks not connected to their parent task. You can identify subtasks in this setting by their little subtask icon on the left of the task name. Useful when you want to focus just on the specifics of subtasks.

For ease of use, make sure you take this into consideration when choosing how you want your subtask view to be displayed:

- Collapsed is good for quick status checking.
- Expanded is helpful for scoping a project's full workflow.
- Separate tasks let you filter and sort subtasks independently without the parent task details.

Which brings us up to **Filters**... which is pretty much ClickUp's hardcore sorting power on top of what we've already talked about in the previous chapters!

Filters bring you such much capability and possibility, I could write a book on its own just for these... idk, maybe someday! ;)

I will get you started with Filters in this chapter, and when you are ready to deep dive - come join the community at askyvi.tips/community and we can nerd all about it!

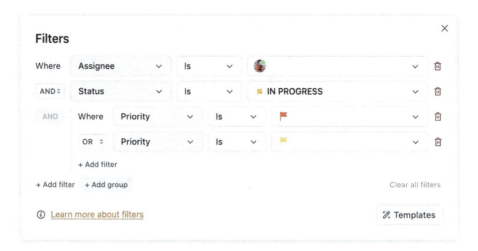

7.3 - ClickUp Custom View Filter Settings

As you can see in *Figure 7.1* when creating filters in ClickUp's custom views, there can only be "AND" or "OR" filters at any given time. You can't directly combine "AND" and "OR" filters together.

However, when you add a + group filter, you now have the capability to combine "AND" and "OR' logic into one filtered view. Here's how it works:

If your **Main filter** is an "AND" filter, you can add a **Group filter** to create "OR" logic. The Group filter lets you choose multiple options from a custom field, which works like an "OR" condition.

For example, you could filter for:

- (Assignee = Me AND Status = In Progress)
- (Group Filter: Priority = High OR Priority = Urgent)

This would show tasks assigned to you that are In Progress, PLUS any tasks marked High or Urgent priority no matter the assignee or status.

The Group filter gives you the flexibility to add "OR" logic when you need it. Just remember that any filters outside the Group filter will follow "AND" logic with each other.

So, while you can't directly combine "AND" and "OR" filters, using Group filters helps add that "OR" capability to open up more possibilities for custom views.

The **Me Mode filter** does exactly as it says... It shows you all the tasks and subtasks assigned to you. It also has a nice little bonus feature. When you are in Me Mode, all tasks you create are automatically assigned to... Yes, you guessed it! YOU!

The **Assignee filter** opens up a menu of all the assignees with tasks assigned to the team. It allows you to easily choose whose assigned tasks you would like to see in the view.

The last one is, **Show closed**, and as the name suggests, this button easily allows you to show closed tasks in your view. It also allows you to choose if you would like to see just closed main tasks or closed subtasks too.

Now that you have a good basic understanding of all things Custom Views - let's take a look at two of my favorite views we use daily before I'll introduce you to some of my favorite Custom View setups, I believe everyone should have in their ClickUp Workspace.

ClickUp Form View

ClickUp's Form View is an incredibly powerful feature that allows you to build customized forms and automatically generate tasks from submissions.

With Form View, you can quickly build forms using a simple drag-and-drop editor right inside your ClickUp workspace. You can include any and nearly all custom field types you already learned about in *Chapter 6*.

Once a form is submitted, the responses turn into tasks and all the information is shown in the custom fields used in your form.. that also happens to show right in that list and therefore the task.

These generated tasks can even be automatically assigned or have a task template attached to bring in additional details. This means your team can spend less time manually creating tasks from submitted information.

The data flows smoothly from form response into structured, actionable tasks ready for your team to execute on. The possibilities are endless!

We use ClickUp forms for client intake questionnaires, research surveys, event registrations, support ticket forms and I'm going to show you how we here at Ask Yvi use it to manage our guest applications for my Boss Your Business Podcast.

- You can see the form in action here: https://askyvi.tips/pod

I trust you won't spam it, or I'll have to turn it off. So, let's not do that!

Adding and editing forms is quite simple.

Add a form view and name it like you learned in *Chapter 1*. Once you've done that, you'll see something like shown in *Figure 7.4*

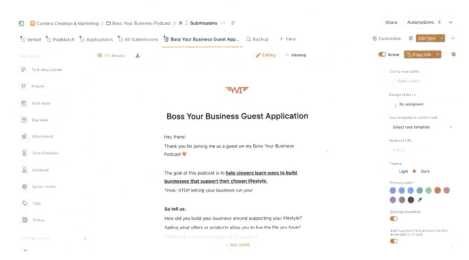

7.4 - ClickUp Form Edit View

This is what you will see when you are in edit view, determined by the button in the top/middle.

On the left-hand side, you'll see a column with all your standard task fields. Right below those you'll see your available custom task fields as well as a button to add new ones.

In the middle, you will see your form.

Simply add your form title, upload an icon, and add a form description as you   wish.

Then drag and drop your task fields from the left into the form to build it.

On the right-hand side you'll see your customization and automation settings.

This is where you can choose to assign the submission tasks to someone or apply a task template when a submission generates a task.

This is also the column where you would choose the color of your form, to add a captcha, or redirect people to another URL after submission.

If you have Business Plus or the Enterprise plan, you also have conditional logic in forms! As you can see in *Figure 7.5*, conditional logic allows you to add additional custom field questions based on the response in a field.

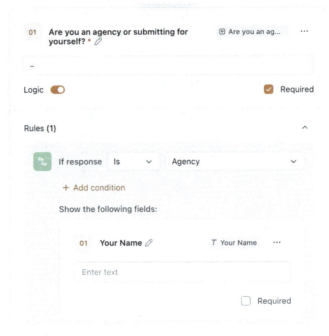

7.5 - ClickUp Form Conditional Logic

Once you are comfortable with ClickUp forms, I'd recommend diving a little deeper into hidden fields!

Hidden fields, and the associated custom URL generated, allow you to predetermine answers in your form.

For example, in our Podcast submission form, we use it to determine where the submission came from.

We are part of the Podmatch community and have a profile on their side. When we get guest requests there, we send a link that has "Podmatch" already chosen, and we know exactly where they came from ;)

More about Hidden Fields on ClickUp's support forum: https://askyvi.tips/CUHidden

And you can see some more use case examples for ClickUp Forms on my YouTube channel right here: https://askyvi.tips/CUForms

Embed View

One of the most missed custom views is the Embed view, which allows you to display content from other web apps directly within your ClickUp workspace.

For example, you could embed a Google Sheet to show a budget, a Canva presentation, or even a Typeform survey (though I'd used ClickUp forms for that). Any web app that provides embedded code can be added!

Embedded views empower you and your team to seamlessly access important information without having to switch between platforms. This helps reduce tool fatigue. Because as useful as your other apps may be, constantly switching between different platforms can diminish productivity and make it hard to see the big picture.

With embedded views, everything comes together in one place - your ClickUp workspace. Some sites like YouTube, Google Sheets & Docs, Google Maps, or Figma can be embedded just by grabbing the share URL and adding it into the first field of your Embed view edit window, as seen in *Figure 7.5.*

Others like Canva, all you need to do is grab the iframe code and enter it into the second field of the edit window.

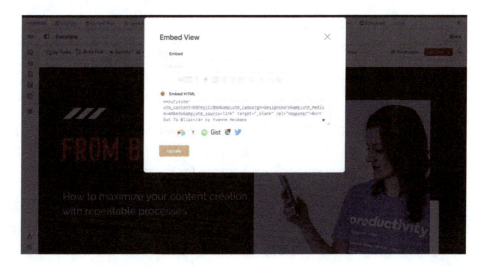

Customizing Views For You

As you already know, custom views allow you to build use case views that match your personal workflow needs. In this section, we'll look at some examples of custom views you can easily create to optimize your own productivity in just minutes:

1. First, we'll set up a "My Tasks" view showing only your assigned tasks ordered by the due date. This gives you a simple snapshot of your   upcoming   workload.

2. Next, we'll build an "On Fire" view to see your highest-priority tasks instantly. This acts like an urgent to-do list when you need to focus   on   critical   projects.

3. Finally, we'll create a social media calendar view to map out when short-form content gets published across platforms. This will help you plan and coordinate a steady stream of posts.

With these customized views tailored specifically for you, it's easy to stay on top of your most important tasks, projects, and publishing schedules.

The options are endless when crafting the perfect views to fit your work style! Let's unlock the potential to take your productivity to the next level.

"My Tasks" Custom View

One of the most useful, and easiest to set up, personal custom views is a simple list of your assigned tasks sorted by due date. This lets you quickly see what's on your plate for the day or week ahead.

The best part is that the "My Tasks" view can be set up once at the workspace level, and then works for every team member without each person having to build the same view themselves.

To build it, first create a new list view at the Everything level and name it "My Tasks."

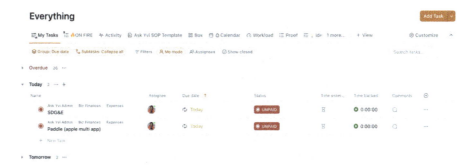

7.7 - ClickUp "My Tasks" Custom View

To filter and sort this view, follow these settings:

- Group: Due Date
- Subtask: Collapse All
- Filters: Choose only if you don't want to see everything
- Me Mode: Turn on
- if you like also sort by the due date to show tasks sorted by time of day

That's it! Now you have a view that extracts just your tasks across all projects and lists them chronologically. It takes seconds to set up but saves you time glancing at your personalized workflow every day.

Because Me Mode is interactive and based on who is looking at it, based on their log-in, this view adapts and shows each of your team members their tasks.

The "My Tasks" view is a perfect example of how custom views can be designed once and then benefit the whole team. Let's look at another useful personal view next - the "On Fire" list for urgent tasks.

On Fire List

When things get hectic, it's critical to identify your most urgent and important tasks that need immediate attention. The "On Fire" custom list view does exactly that - it acts as an urgent to-do list by highlighting your top priority tasks across projects.

To build the On Fire List, first create a new list view at the Everything level. This ensures it pulls in top-priority tasks from ALL spaces, folders, and lists. But this also means it's only available to full members, not guests! However, you can recreate this in a dashboard too, using the same group and filter settings.

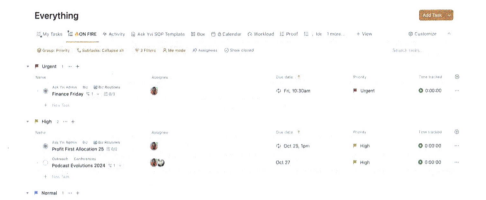

7.8 - ClickUp "On Fire" Custom View

To recreate this Custom List view, follow these settings:

- Group: Priority
- Subtasks: Collapse all (or your personal choice)
- Filter: Location is (not) based on your preference
  Due Date is set
- Me Mode: on
- Sort by: Due Date column

Now every one of your team members knows exactly what fire they should put out first before even working on their other tasks.. no need to slack them or be all like *"Aaahhh, the client is crazy. Did you do the thing?!"*

I mean, of course they won't miss it because it's been marked HIGH priority, and it's gonna be the first thing they see when they login to ClickUp and start their shift!

In this video I show you how the My Task View and On Fire List work: https://askyvi.tips/CUFire

So many Custom View Possibilities

There are endless possibilities as far as ClickUp custom views are concerned. We've only just scratched the surface looking at a few examples like the My Tasks view, On Fire list, and embedded views.

On my YouTube channel, you can find many more examples of custom views to optimize your productivity, organization, reporting, and more.

Remember, many of these can also be set up and used in Dashboards!

A few ideas to spark your imagination:

- Daily standup view showing tasks from yesterday, today, and blocked tasks.
- Content calendar view for planning and tracking publishes across platforms.
- Manage 100s of Reels: https://askyvi.tips/CVReels

And even more use cases on my YouTube channel: https://askyvi.tips/youtube

Think about your unique workflow needs and how custom views could provide the perfect perspective. The options are limitless for crafting views that fit your style and supercharge your team's productivity.

And that wraps up our journey through **Mastering The Basics of ClickUp**!

By now, you should have a strong understanding of ClickUp's main features and capabilities. We've covered everything from the hierarchy and layout to notifications, custom fields, custom views, and best practices.

You're equipped with the core knowledge to start using ClickUp efficiently for your personal productivity or team project management.

Of course, there's always more to explore! As you spend time in ClickUp, think about which features could be most helpful for your needs. Consult the ClickUp Help Center, check out my YouTube channel, or pop into my S.O.A.R.R. Community when questions arise.

Most importantly, don't feel pressured to implement everything at once. Grow your ClickUp skills steadily over time. Start with the basics like building out your structure, and then add custom fields and views as needed.

The goal is to shape ClickUp into the perfect productivity engine for YOU. Let it adapt to your working style rather than trying to overhaul everything instantly!

I'm so proud of you. Thank you so much for joining me on this ClickUp journey! I hope you feel empowered to unlock ClickUp's possibilities and transform your efficiency. Keep learning, customizing, and leveraging ClickUp to accomplish great things.

The future is productive!

www.ingramcontent.com/pod-product-compliance
Lightning Source LLC
LaVergne TN
LVHW081528050326
832903LV00025B/1677